Reserve Requirements in the Brave New
Macroprudential World

A WORLD BANK STUDY

Reserve Requirements in the Brave New Macroprudential World

Tito Cordella, Pablo M. Federico,
Carlos A. Vegh, and Guillermo Vuletin

THE WORLD BANK
Washington, D.C.

BROOKINGS GLOBAL | CERES
B Economic and
Social Policy in
Latin America
Initiative

Contents

Boxes

Figures

Tables

Preface

Reserve Requirements in the Brave new Macroprudential World summarizes the main policy conclusions of a regional study sponsored by the Chief Economist Office of the Latin American Region of the World Bank. The study was conducted by a team composed by Tito Cordella, Augusto de la Torre, Pablo Federico, Alain Ize, Samuel Pienknagura, Carlos Vegh, and Guillermo Vuletin. Excellent advice has been received from our peer reviewers Eva Gutierrez, Luis Jacome, and Andrew Powell. We would also like to thank participants at conferences/seminars at the Bank of Spain, Central Bank of Turkey, CEMLA, Central Bank of Uruguay, IDB, and IMF for very insightful comments and suggestions, and Gabriela Calderon Motta and James Trevino for excellent editorial assistance.

Acknowledgments

This is a joint research paper by the World Bank and the Brookings Global-CERES Economic and Social Policy in Latin America Initiative.

About the Brookings-Global CERES Economic and Social Policy in Latin America Initiative:

The Brookings Global-CERES Economic and Social Policy in Latin America Initiative (ESPLA) is a partnership between the Global Economy and Development Program at Brookings and the Center for the Study of Economic and Social Affairs (CERES) in Montevideo, Uruguay. The initiative aims at producing high-quality, independent, debate-shaping analysis and research on economic and social policies in Latin America. ESPLA's core research agenda focuses on macroeconomic policy, social policy, governance and well-being metrics. For more information about ESPLA, please visit http://www.brookings.edu/espla

B | BROOKINGS GLOBAL | CERES
Economic and
Social Policy in
Latin America
Initiative

About the Authors

Tito Cordella is a lead economist in the World Bank Development Economics Group (DEC). Before joining the Bank, he worked at the International Monetary Fund, alternating operational and research activities. He has published widely in trade, banking, and international finance/development. He previously taught at Pompeu Fabra University in Barcelona and at the University of Bologna. An Italian national, he holds a PhD in economics from the Université Catholique de Louvain, Belgium (European Doctoral Program).

Pablo M. Federico is a member of BlackRock's Global Market Strategies Group (GMSG), a systematic global macro hedge fund. He is responsible for research and development of currency and fixed income models within GMSG, with a special focus on emerging markets. Prior to joining BlackRock in 2012, Dr. Federico was a consultant to the World Bank Group, the International Monetary Fund, and the Inter-American Development Bank. Previously, he was a research analyst with LECG, where he built company valuation models. Dr. Federico earned a BS in economics from Universidad del CEMA in 2004 and a PhD in economics from The University of Maryland in 2012.

Carlos A. Vegh is the Fred H. Sanderson Professor of International Economics at Johns Hopkins University, where he holds appointments at the School of Advanced International Studies and the Economics Department. He is also a Research Associate at the National Bureau of Economic Research and a Non-Resident Senior Fellow at the Brookings Institution. He received his PhD in Economics from the University of Chicago in 1987. He spent the early years of his career at the International Monetary Fund's Research Department. From 1995 to 2013, he was a tenured professor first at UCLA and then at the University of Maryland. He has been co-editor of the *Journal of International Economics* and the *Journal of Development Economics*, the leading journals in their respective fields. He has published extensively in leading academic journals on monetary and fiscal policy in developing and emerging countries. He has co-edited a volume in honor of Guillermo Calvo (MIT Press) and recently published a graduate textbook on open economy macroeconomics for developing countries (MIT Press).

Guillermo Vuletin is a fellow in the Brookings Global-CERES Economic and Social Policy in Latin America Initiative. He is also a visiting professor at The Johns Hopkins School of Advanced International Studies. His research focuses on fiscal and monetary policies with a particular interest in macroeconomic policy in emerging and developing countries.

Abbreviations

DSGE	Dynamic Stochastic General Equilibrium
ECB	European Central Bank
GDP	gross domestic product
IFI	international financial institution
IMF	International Monetary Fund
LTV	loan to value ratio
RGDP	real gross domestic product
RR	reserve requirements
RRP	reserve requirement policy
VAR	vector autoregression analysis

Executive Summary

Motivation

The active use of prudential instruments to regulate the level of credit and influence its allocation, popular in the 1970s and 1980s, fell somehow into disgrace in the 1990s, when the regulatory pendulum swung towards liberalization as a way to foster financial deepening and a more efficient allocation of resources. In the late 2000s, however, as the global financial crisis hit financially developed economies with a vengeance, the pendulum swung back towards more regulation and a much more active use of prudential instruments—such as reserve requirements, loan to value ratios, taxes on credit, and capital requirements—to smooth out the credit cycle and avert major crises. Macroprudential policy, to use the current jargon, thus gained momentum and became the policy buzzword of the post-Lehman world.

It is important to recognize that there may be two different reasons why macroprudential policies are so popular nowadays. The first, fashionable in academic circles and international financial institutions (IFIs), focuses on the buildup of systemic risk and is driven by financial stability concerns. The second, more popular among policy makers in emerging markets, focuses on macroeconomic stabilization in the presence of large capital flows and is driven mostly by the desire to stabilize the exchange rate and the credit cycle.

In terms of systemic risk-driven macroprudential policy, the unfolding of the subprime crisis brought to the forefront the potentially dangerous links between macroeconomic and financial stability and the limitations of central bank policy frameworks that may rely on a single instrument, the interest rate, to deal simultaneously with distinct real and financial objectives. John Taylor's well-known critique to the effect that the Federal Funds rate was too low in the mid-2000's and was a major contributing factor to the housing bubble and its subsequent collapse is an illustration of how monetary policy may inadvertently lead to major financial instabilities and systemic risk problems which, in theory at least, could have been prevented by a more active use of systemic risk-driven macroprudential policy.[1]

In turn, the rebirth of business cycle-driven macroprudential policy is also linked to the global crisis, albeit indirectly, through the extreme monetary easing that followed the financial meltdowns in industrial countries. Indeed, the abundant liquidity provided by the Federal Reserve, the European Central Bank (ECB), and the Bank of Japan triggered a frantic search for higher yields that pushed capital flows into emerging countries,[2] and the talk of its tapering to a sudden capital flows reversal. Even if the medium and long-run benefits of an open capital account in terms of investment and growth are well-known, so are the major macroeconomic-management problems that it poses in the short term by leading to an overheating of the economy, large real appreciation, and higher inflation, all of which may eventually come to a screeching halt (the so-called sudden stop). In other words, central banks that can only rely on a short-term policy rate are faced with serious policy dilemmas: (i) in good times, raising interest rates to cool down the economy makes carry-trade even more attractive, thus exacerbating the capital inflows problems and appreciating further the domestic currency; (ii) in bad times, lowering interest rates to stimulate the economy leads to additional capital outflows which further depreciate the currency; (iii) in both situations, leaving interest rates unchanged or adjusting them procyclically may help in controlling capital flows and keeping stable the value of the domestic currency but at the cost of current and future inflation in good times or a worsening of the downturns in bad ones. It is in these all-too-common policy scenarios that the use of prudential tools can help the monetary authorities in smoothing the capital flow/credit cycle without losing control of the currency.

In practice, the distinction between systemic risk-driven and business cycle-driven use of macroprudential policy is, of course, not a stark one. Systemic-risk macroprudential policy can contribute to macroeconomic stabilization by reducing the amplitude of the credit cycle (the dynamic provision measures implemented in Spain would be a good example) and the business cycle-driven use of macroprudential policy can certainly contribute to financial stability by preventing excessive (or suboptimal) fluctuations in capital flows, which may reduce the probability of systemic risk.

While this report will not be able to distinguish between the two different drivers of macroprudential policies, it will focus mainly on the business cycle-driven use of macroprudential policy and provide arguments supporting the predominance of macroeconomic stabilization considerations.[3] While we can certainly not rule out *a priori* that systemic-risk macroprudential policy may also be related to the business cycle to the extent that the risk cycle (assuming such a concept can be well defined and measured) may be correlated with the business cycle, we will take the position that the use of macroprudential policy linked to the business cycle is primarily driven by macroeconomic stabilization considerations. Furthermore—and while there is a number of different prudential instruments that have and could be used by monetary authorities—we will focus exclusively on reserve requirements (RRs) for two reasons. First, RR are the most widely used prudential instrument to deal with business cycle concerns. Second—and to be as substantive and novel as possible—we wanted our analysis to be based on long and comparable time series for a large number of countries, both industrial and developing, and RR are the only instrument for which it was possible (although not without a lot of hard work!) to put together such an extensive and novel dataset.

Main Findings

For the purposes of this policy report, we have put together a dataset on quarterly *legal* reserve requirement rates for 52 countries (15 industrial and 37 developing countries) for the period 1970–2011.[4] This novel dataset, together with more readily available data on credit, international reserves, gross domestic product (GDP), and other macroeconomic series, allows us to identify a series of stylized facts regarding the use over time of RR as a macrostabilization tool.

Our first step is to distinguish between those countries that have actively used RR and those that have not. To this end, we compare the frequency of changes in RR with the average duration of the business cycle and classify as active any country that changes RR more than once within the business cycle. We find a striking difference between developing and industrial countries: 68 percent of developing countries are classified as active, compared to just 33 percent of industrial countries. This difference becomes even more dramatic if we focus on the post-2004 period, as there is not a single industrial country that has pursed active RR policy. This clearly suggests that while RR has not been used as a macroprudential tool in industrial countries, many developing countries have used RR as a second policy instrument (that is, in addition to monetary policy). In fact, in the post-2004 period, 90 percent of active developing countries have used RR countercyclically (that is, raising legal reserve requirements in good times and lowering them in bad times), strongly indicating their use as a macroeconomic stabilization tool. Further, we find that, among active developing countries, the higher the level of the credit to GDP ratio, the more countercyclical has been the use of RR (even after controlling for the level of GDP).

We then study in detail the links between monetary policy and RR policy. We first document the dramatic difference between industrial and developing countries when it comes to monetary policy (that is, interest rate policy). While every single industrial country has pursued countercyclical monetary policy during the period under study, only 59 percent of developing countries have done so. We show evidence that suggests that this difference is due to the fact that developing countries are hesitant to raise interest rates in good times for fear of attracting more capital inflows and further appreciating the currency. Conversely, in bad times, they are hesitant to lower interest rates for fear of seeing their currency plummet. It is precisely the fact that the policy interest rate is tied to an exchange rate objective that induces developing countries to use RR countercyclically. In other words, they use RR to do the work that the policy interest rate cannot or will not do.

We also show how foreign exchange market intervention is used heavily by developing countries to prevent currency appreciation (depreciation) in good (bad) times. In other words, traditionally, the most typical policy mix for developing countries in bad times has been to raise interest rates and sell international reserves (to defend the currency) and lower RR to spur the economy. The opposite policy mix, lower (or at least not increase) interest rates, buying foreign currency, and increasing RR has been the typical policy mix in good times.

In sum, the evidence just discussed suggests that RR have been an extremely common policy tool in the hands of emerging markets' policy makers eager to stabilize the capital flow/credit cycle to avoid excessive volatility but who prefer not to rely solely on interest rates for those purposes. Not surprisingly, RR have been used more actively in countries with an open capital account, more prone to currency crises, and exhibiting a procyclical currency (that is, a currency that depreciates in bad times and appreciates in good times), all of which puts severe limits on monetary policy's ability to smooth out the level of credit and/or economic activity. All this evidence is consistent with the use of macroprudential policies as a macrostabilization tool.

The Unintended Consequences of RR Policy

The report shows that tightening reserve requirements in good times smoothes out credit volumes, thereby stabilizing the business cycle. But how does it affect individual banks' risk-taking incentives? The short answer is that (unlike other prudential instruments such as capital requirements) an increase in RR may well increase banks' risk-taking behavior.[5]

The reason is that an increase in banks' external cost of funding, such as obligations to depositors, may exacerbate the moral hazard problems associated with limited liabilities and induce banks to behave in a less prudent way. This does not mean that RR are bad instruments *per se*. Quite to the contrary—and as we have shown in this report—they are powerful macrostabilization tools that have helped monetary policy in the presence of large and volatile capital flows. In addition, in combination with other prudential measures that target the banks' liability structure, RR can strengthen the financial system's resilience to liquidity shocks. Rather, our point is to stress that there can be a trade-off between certain prudential instruments in the sense that they are able to smooth out the credit/business cycle and hence also reduce aggregate/systemic risk and yet they may have negative consequences on individual banks' risk-taking incentives.

We conclude that it is important for policy makers to take into account the possible microeconomic consequences (such as risk taking) of business cycle-driven macroprudential policy. This is certainly an area that has received little, if any, attention. Even systemic risk-driven macroprudential policies aimed at reducing financial externalities may, under certain circumstances, increase banks' risk appetite so that macroprudential policies may end up having results that may partially undo their intended effects.

Policy Tensions and Trade-offs

Finally, we emphasize that the overall design of macroprudential policies should start from a careful analysis of the role that different financial frictions play in different environments (or in different moments of the business cycle). Given that similar symptoms can reflect very different underlying forces, suitable policy responses require a reasonable sense of what is behind the observed financial turbulence, whether the inefficiencies are mainly driven by policy failures or market failures and, in the latter case, whether the relevant market failures reflect mainly public moral hazard, substantial externalities that rational players do not internalize, or irrational mood swings driven by noise traders. Finding a proper balance in macroprudential policy is further complicated by tensions and trade-offs in policy impacts when different kind of financial frictions occur simultaneously.

Given these constraints, two broad macroprudential policy options can be envisaged. One option is to assemble an all-terrain regulatory framework. The alternative is to develop a state-contingent (bimodal) regulatory framework that focuses in normal times on market discipline and the classic agency frictions but shifts in exceptional times (of bubble formation or bubble bursts) to a focus on systemic risk and the destabilizing role of collective action and cognition frictions.

Progress towards bridging the gap between theory and practice will therefore require better identifying the main frictions and failures at work, formally incorporating them in theoretical models, assessing their welfare impact, and sorting out constrained efficiencies from constrained inefficiencies. This effort will need to be accompanied by further empirical efforts to estimate and calibrate the net impact of regulations, while at the same time gauging their unintended side effects.

Conclusions and Policy Lessons
Several important conclusions and policy lessons follow from this report:

- We find a very different behavior in industrial and emerging countries regarding the use of macroprudential policy (at least in terms of RR). Since 2004 no industrial country has resorted to active RR policy, whereas close to half of developing countries have, of which 90 percent have used RR countercyclically.
- RR seem to be an important component of a trio of policy instruments (together with short-term interest rates and foreign exchange market intervention) that developing countries have relied on for several decades now, as they go through boom-bust cycles mainly induced by international capital flows. Despite all the buzz about systemic risk-driven macroprudential policy, we found no evidence of such use of RR in industrial countries.
- The genesis for resorting to RR lies essentially on the behavior of the exchange rate over the business cycle in developing countries (with the currency depreciating in bad times and appreciating in good times). This complicates enormously the use of interest rates as a countercyclical instrument because doing so would appreciate (depreciate) even more the currency in good (bad) times.

- The evidence suggests that RR are an effective instrument (that is, a rise in RR increases the interest rate spread and reduces credit and GDP) that can well be used countercyclically when concerns about the effects of interest rates on the exchange rate become paramount.
- It may well be the case—and this is what we observe in countries such as Chile where policy institutions have improved steadily over time—that developing countries may reach a point in time where it may no longer be necessary to use RR as a business cycle-driven macroprudential policy. Until then, however, RR seem to be a natural and effective instrument to complement monetary policy.
- Even if and when a given developing country may reach a point where RR are no longer necessary as a part of the policy mix, RR may still be optimal to use as systemic risk-driven macroprudential policy. Our report, however, does not speak to the effectiveness of RR as a risk-reducing prudential instrument and therefore future research is called for in this regard.
- While from a macroprudential point of view, the most common prudential instruments are essentially equivalent (for instance, RR, capital requirements, and taxes on credit), from a microprudential point of view they may elicit very different responses regarding banks' risk-taking behavior over the business cycle.
- Depending on the nature and the drivers of the business cycle, conflicts may arise between the micro- and macroprudential policy stances.
- The overall design of macroprudential policies should follow a careful analysis of the role that different financial frictions play in different environments since similar symptoms can reflect very different underlying forces.
- More research is needed to embed banks' risk-taking incentives in macro models so as to be able to properly assess and quantify the tensions that may arise between macro- and macroprudential policies and to design a coherent prudential framework for the financial system.

Notes

1. More generally, as discussed in de la Torre and Ize (2013), systemic-risk macroprudential policy would comprise, among others, measures aimed at offsetting the moral hazard implications of postcrises interventions, keeping principal-agent and social and private incentives aligned along the business cycle, and tempering mood-swing-based financial excesses.
2. Guido Mantega, Brazilian finance minister, famously referred to these policies as currency wars, which would force emerging countries to deal with large capital inflows and appreciating currencies.
3. Needless to say, by doing so, we do not mean to diminish in any way the importance of systemic risk-driven macroprudential policy. Our goal, however, was to approach the subject of macroprudential policy from a strictly

macroeconomic stabilization point of view, an angle that has received relatively little attention in the academic literature.

4. We focus on the legal reserve requirement rate because it is a policy tool, as opposed to effective reserve requirements, which are an outcome greatly influenced by deposit fluctuations over the business cycle.

5. Of course, the more typical cost of using RR is that they constitute a tax on financial intermediation. But this concept really applies to the *level*, rather than the cyclical variation of RR around that level. We see the determination of the optimal level of RR as falling outside the scope of our analysis.

CHAPTER 1

Introduction

In the aftermath of the global financial crisis of 2008–09, macroprudential policy has become the new policy buzzword. Indeed, it seems hard to find any detailed statement about macroeconomic policy—particularly relating to emerging countries—that does not include, at some point or another, some reference to financial stability or systemic risk and the resulting need for "macroprudential policy."

Moreover, in the last few years the debate on the consequences of quantitative easing (and its tapering) by the industrial world (particularly the United States) and the ensuing "currency wars" put macroprudential policy, in the form of changes in reserve requirements, at the forefront of policy discussions. For example, in a February 12, 2013, article, the *Financial Times* focuses on the macroeconomic problems that appreciating currencies have brought about in several Latin American countries and notices that while Chile, Colombia, and Peru have eschewed Brazilian-style capital controls, "they have turned to direct foreign currency intervention; paying down foreign debt; macroprudential measures such as increases in bank reserve requirements and interest rate cuts that reduce the 'carry,' or interest rate differential, for yield hungry investors."[1] In other words, changes in reserve requirements are very much part of the main policy menu at the disposal of emerging market policy makers concerned about how to respond to capital inflows or outflows.

Indeed, when the appeal of emerging markets started to wane last summer and their currencies consequently began to plummet, opposite kinds of measures were undertaken. Brazil cut its tax on overseas investment in domestic bonds from 6 percent to zero, the Indian government relaxed overseas borrowing rules, and forex interventions to defend currencies became widespread. It is not hard to predict that other macroprudential measures such as reserve requirements will soon be adjusted to this new environment.

However, as a French saying rightly reminds us, *plus ça change, plus c'est la même chose* (the more things change, the more they remain the same). In a widely cited 1993 article in the *IMF Staff Papers* on capital inflows to Latin American in the early 1990s, Calvo, Leiderman, and Reinhart discuss in detail the policies deployed by policy makers in the region and conclude that "there are grounds to support a mix of policy intervention based on the imposition of a tax on short-term capital inflows, on enhancing the flexibility of exchange rates, and on raising marginal reserve requirements on short-term bank deposits." And, even earlier, in his celebrated 1985 paper "Good-bye financial repression, hello financial crash," Diaz-Alejandro had already entertained the possibility that "prudential regulatory machinery could be used to discourage volatile international financial flows [by] relying primarily on taxes or tax-like requirements, that is, via special reserve requirements for certain types of unwanted international financial transactions."

In terms of the broader policy discussion on macroprudential policy, it is important to recognize that there seems to be two different reasons why macroprudential policies are so popular nowadays. The first, fashionable in academic circles and international financial institution (IFIs), focuses on the buildup of systemic risk and is driven by financial stability concerns. The second—already mentioned above and more popular among policy makers in emerging markets— focuses on macroeconomic stabilization in the presence of large capital flows and is driven mostly by the desire to stabilize the exchange rate and the credit cycle. In practice, the distinction between the systemic risk-driven and the business-cycle driven use of macroprudential policy is not a stark one. Macroprudential policies aimed at dealing with systemic risk can contribute to macroeconomic stabilization by reducing the amplitude of the credit cycle (the dynamic provision measures implemented in Spain are a good example), and the use of macroprudential instruments to deal with the business cycle can certainly contribute to financial stability by preventing excessive (or "suboptimal") fluctuations in capital flows, which may reduce the probability of systemic risk.

While this report will not be able to distinguish between the two different drivers of macroprudential policies, it will focus mainly on the use of business cycle-driven macroprudential policy and will provide arguments supporting the predominance of macroeconomic stabilization considerations.[2] Further, even though we can certainly not rule out *a priori* that systemic-risk macroprudential policy may also be related to the business cycle to the extent that the "risk cycle" (assuming such a concept can be well defined and measured) may be correlated with the business cycle, we will take the position that the use of macroprudential policy linked to the business cycle is primarily driven by macroeconomic stabilization considerations. In addition, we will focus exclusively on reserve requirements (RR) for two reasons. First, RR are the most widely used prudential instrument to deal with business cycle concerns and have a long history in the region and elsewhere.[3] In fact, ever since the financial liberalization of the late 1970s in the Southern-Cone, each new wave of capital inflows into the region (either due to financial liberalization or following a period of outflows) has triggered a remarkably similar discussion regarding the pros and cons of higher reserve requirements.[4] Second—and to be as substantive and novel as possible—we wanted our analysis to be based on long and comparable time series for a large number of countries, both industrial and developing, and RR are the only instrument for which it was possible (although not without a lot of hard work!) to put together such an extensive and novel dataset.

To this effect, we have put together a dataset on quarterly *legal* reserve requirements for 52 countries (15 industrial and 37 developing countries) for the period 1970–2011.[5] This novel dataset, together with more readily available data on credit, international reserves, gross domestic product (GDP), and other macroeconomic series will allow us to identify a series of stylized facts regarding the use over time of RR as a macroeconomic stabilization tool. Based on these stylized facts, we can then proceed to provide a policy rationalization for what we have observed and for the relation between reserve requirement policies (RRP), monetary policy, and foreign exchange market intervention.

This policy report proceeds as follows. Based on Federico, Vegh, and Vuletin (2013a), chapter 2 documents the key stylized facts regarding the use of reserve requirements as a macroeconomic stabilization tool and how RRP relates to the level of credit, monetary policy, and foreign exchange market intervention. We first propose an operational definition to distinguish countries that make use of RR as a stabilization tool (which we dubbed "active countries") from those that do not ("passive countries"). We show that developing countries are much more likely to pursue an active RRP than industrial countries. This is particularly true in the post-2004 period, which is consistent with the casual observation of the increasing reliance on macroprudential policy in emerging markets. We then show that, within active countries, the level of credit to GDP is an important determinant of how countercyclical is the use of RR.

We then analyze the relation of RRP with monetary policy. Our starting observation is the fact that, unlike industrial countries, many emerging markets have not used interest rates countercyclically (that is, to smooth out the business cycle). We will interpret this as reflecting the need to defend the currency in bad times (for fear of a sudden and perilous depreciation) and the fear of attracting yet more capital inflows in good times (by making domestic-currency assets more attractive). In order to understand the simultaneous choice of RRP and monetary policy, we then build what we call "policy mix matrices" to illustrate all the possible combinations of RRP and monetary policy in terms of their cyclical properties (procyclical, acyclical, and countercyclical). We show how industrial countries typically make no use of RR and conduct countercyclical monetary policy. Emerging markets, in contrast, rely heavily on RRP and often use it as a substitute for monetary policy, in the sense of using RRP to smooth the business cycle and using interest rate policy either acyclically or procyclically.

We then examine the use of foreign exchange market intervention as an additional policy tool and how it interacts with RRP. We find that, by and large, foreign exchange market intervention is used to smooth out changes in the nominal exchange rate by buying foreign assets in good times (thus preventing "excessive" currency appreciation) and selling foreign assets in bad times (thus preventing "excessive" currency depreciation).

In chapter 3, we use four Latin America and the Caribbean countries to simulate the policy response to output and exchange rate shocks. The picture that emerges is one in which in bad times developing countries choose a policy mix that consists on increasing interest rates (to defend the currency), selling international reserves (also to defend the currency), and lowering reserve requirements (to stimulate credit and, hence, economic activity). Conversely, in good times countries tend to accumulate international reserves (to fight off appreciation of the domestic currency), increase RR to cool off the credit cycle, but are reluctant to increase interest rate because of the fear of exacerbating capital inflows.

Chapter 4 attempts to provide a policy rationale for the stylized facts we identified in the previous sections. In our view of the world, the distinctive feature of emerging markets' business cycle is the fact that domestic currencies tend to appreciate in good times and depreciate (and often precipitously) in bad times. A sharp currency depreciation in bad times leaves policy makers with little choice but to increase interest rates (or at least not lower them) to make domestic-currency assets more attractive and prevent the currency from plummeting. This procyclical monetary policy triggers the need for a second instrument that can be used to stimulate output. In this context, lowering RR should help in fostering credit expansion and thus steer the economy out of recession.

A critical issue—often ignored in policy as well as in the academic circles—is the possible (often unintended) consequences of different macroprudential instruments on individual banks' risk-taking incentives. In chapter 5, we argue that if from a macroprudential point of view, different instruments—such as RR, capital requirements, and taxes on credit—may be equivalent, from a microprudential point of view, generally, they are not. In addition, depending on what the drivers of the business cycle are, the macro and microprudential stances may or may not go hand in hand. Chapter 6 elaborates on the possible tensions between different policy objectives and maintains that policy makers may disregard the microeconomic consequences of different macroprudential instruments only at their own peril. The main policy implications of the report are summarized in chapter 7.

Notes

1. John Paul Rothbone, "Currency Fears Spread in Latin America", *Financial Times*, February 12, 2013.

2. Needless to say, by so doing, we do not mean to diminish in any way the importance of systemic risk-driven macroprudential policy. Our goal, however, was to approach the subject of macroprudential policy from a strictly macroeconomic stabilization point of view, an angle that has received relatively little attention in the academic literature.

3. See Federico, Vegh, and Vuletin (2013c) for an analysis of 40 years of macroprudential policy history in Brazil and Mexico. They document that while a wide variety of macroprudential instruments were used over time in both countries, RR were the most common. One may question whether the use of RR should be viewed as macroprudential policy rather than monetary policy. In our view of the world, this would depend on policy makers' intentions. If RR are used exclusively to regulate market liquidity, they should indeed be viewed as monetary policy. If, instead, they are used

Reserve Requirements in the Brave New Macroprudential World
http://dx.doi.org/10.1596/978-1-4648-0212-6

to influence risk taking over the business cycle, they should be viewed as macroprudential policy. While interesting, this distinction is not relevant for our empirically
based analysis since we do not observe policy makers' intentions. We thus take the
implicit position—consistent with common practice—that changes in RR indeed
constitute as a "macroprudential policy."

4. Of course, the use of reserve requirements as a macroeconomic stabilization tool
   should not be confused with their use as a tool of *financial repression* in the preceding
   decades, as discussed in detail in the classical analyses of McKinnon (1973) and Shaw
   (1973). In this case, high reserve requirements, together with interest rate ceilings,
   quantitative restrictions on credit allocation, multiple exchange rates, and other non-
   market mechanisms were part of a financial repression model, which by depressing
   savings and investment, led to dismal growth and overall economic performance. Of
   course, the financial liberalization of the 1960s and 1970s in Latin American brought
   its own set of financial problems, as masterfully discussed by Diaz-Alejandro (1985),
   which arguably endure until today.

5. For convenience, we will use the term "countries" but notice that our list includes the
   Euro zone as a single economic unit and Ecuador as two distinct economic units
   (before and after full dollarization in the year 2000). The reader is referred to
   Federico, Vegh, and Vuletin (2013a) for the list of countries, sample periods, and data
   sources. Notice that we are interested in the *legal* reserve requirement rate as opposed
   to the *effective* or *average* reserve requirements because the latter would be highly
   sensitive to the business cycle (as deposits correlate positively with the business cycle)
   and would thus not be a good indicator of the cyclical stance of reserve requirement
   policy.

Reserve Requirements in the Brave New Macroprudential World
http://dx.doi.org/10.1596/978-1-4648-0212-6

CHAPTER 2

Stylized Facts

This chapter identifies the main stylized facts related to the use of reserve requirements as a macroeconomic stabilization tool. We first develop an operational definition that will allow us to establish which countries have indeed used reserve requirements as a macroeconomic stabilization tool. We then look at the relation between reserve requirement policy (RRP) and monetary policy. Finally, we look at the relation between RRP and foreign exchange market intervention.

Which Countries Have Used Reserve Requirements as a Macroeconomic Stabilization Tool?

This is the first question that one would like to answer since, unlike monetary or fiscal policy, not all countries may have necessarily used reserve requirements to smooth out the business cycle. Answering this question, however, requires some operational definition of what do we mean by using reserve requirements as a macroeconomic stabilization tool. The main idea behind our operational definition will be that if the average duration between the changes in reserve requirements (RR) for any given country is shorter than the average duration of the business cycle in the same country, we will classify that country as having an active RRP. If not, we will classify that country as having a passive RRP.[1] For example, suppose that, on average, a country changes reserve requirements every 10 years but the average duration of its business cycle is 3 years. Clearly, such a country is not using reserve requirements to influence the business cycle. Conversely, suppose that reserve requirements are changed every two quarters with the same average duration of the business cycle. In this case, it is very likely that the main purpose of changing reserve requirements is to smooth out the business cycle.[2]

Figure 2.1 shows the quarterly frequency of changes in legal reserve requirements (RRs) for each of the 52 countries in our sample for the period 1970–2011 (notice that duration is simply the inverse of frequency). Yellow bars indicate developing countries while black bars denote industrial countries. For example, if a country has a frequency of 0.5, this means that it changes RR once every two quarters. In other words, the average duration between changes in RR

Figure 2.1 Frequency of Changes in Reserve Requirements (1970–2011)

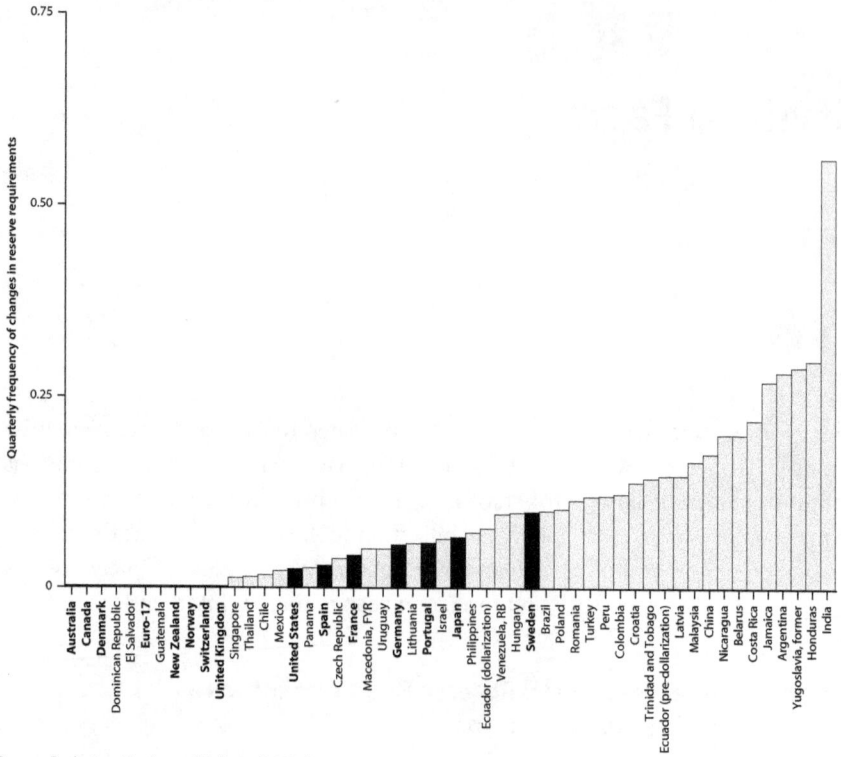

Source: Federico, Vegh, and Vuletin (2013a).

is two quarters (1/0.5). As the figure makes clear, developing countries exhibit the highest frequencies. In fact, the industrial country with the highest frequency, Sweden, has a frequency of 0.10 indicating that it changes RR once every 10 quarters (or 2.5 years). From figure 2.1, we can already guess that, under our operational definition, many more developing than industrial countries will be classified as having an active RRP.

Figure 2.2 shows the classification of all countries in the sample into active or passive when it comes to RRP. To this effect, we construct a scatter plot with the vertical axis indicating the average time (in years) between changes in RR and the horizontal axis indicating the average duration of the business cycle (also in years). We then draw a 45-degree line. Generally speaking, countries below the 45-degree line are "active" countries because the average time between changes is lower than the average duration of the business cycle. Conversely, countries above the 45-degree line are passive countries.[3]

Based on figure 2.2, 62 percent of countries (32 out of 52) are classified as active countries. As expected, there is a striking difference between developing and industrial countries: 68 percent (or 27 out of 37) of developing countries are classified as active, whereas only 33 percent of industrial countries (5 out of 15) are classified as active. In the case of Latin America and the Caribbean countries, 65 percent (or 11 out of 17) are classified as active.

Figure 2.2 Active versus Passive Reserve Requirement Policy (1970–2011)

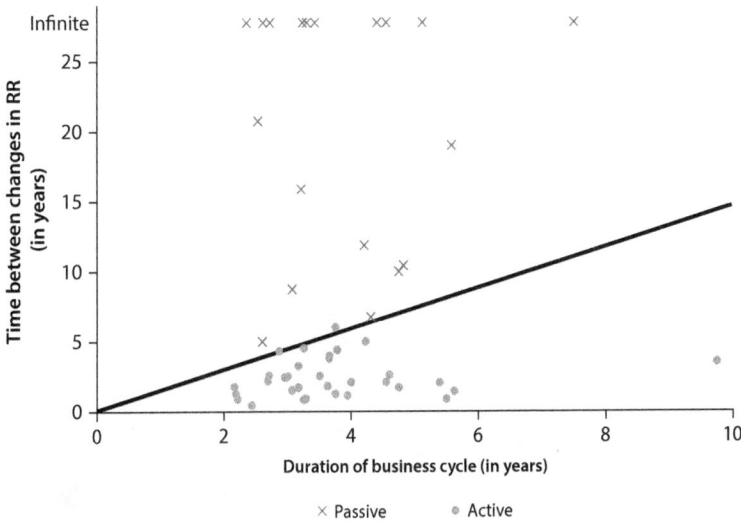

Source: Federico, Vegh, and Vuletin (2013a).

Note: The dashed line is a 45-degree line. Countries located below (above) the 45-degree line are countries for which the change in reserve requirements takes place, on average, at least (less than) one time per business cycle. Countries are classified as active if the average duration of business cycle plus one standard deviation of business cycle is larger than the average time between changes in reserve requirements. RR indicates reserve requirements.

In fact, the difference between industrial and developing countries becomes even more striking if we divide the sample before and after 2004. For the post-2004 sample—and as figure 2.3 illustrates—while the frequency of changes in RR for developing countries looks roughly similar to the whole sample (figure 2.1), there is not a single industrial country that has changed legal reserve requirements in this period.[4] Using our formal criterion, 57 percent of developing countries (or 21 out of 37) are classified as active in the 2005–11 period.

What Have Been the Cyclical Properties of RR as a Macroeconomic Stabilization Tool?

Now that we have identified a group of countries that have used RRP actively during the 1970–2011 period, we look into the cyclical properties of RR in these countries. In other words, we would like to know if RR have had a positive or negative correlation with the business cycle.

To this effect, we compute the correlation between the cyclical components of RR and real gross domestic product (GDP) for each of the 32 countries classified as active. These correlations are illustrated in figure 2.4. We can see that 72 percent (or 23 out 32) of the correlations are positive, indicating countercyclical RRP.[5] If we limit ourselves to positive correlations that are significantly different from zero, the figure accounts for 38 percent (or 12 out of 32).

As we already mentioned, however, the figures for the whole sample period mask an important relative change. Dividing the sample again before and after 2004 (figure 2.5, Panels a and b, respectively), we can see that before 2005, the

Figure 2.3 Frequency of Changes in Reserve Requirements (2005–11)

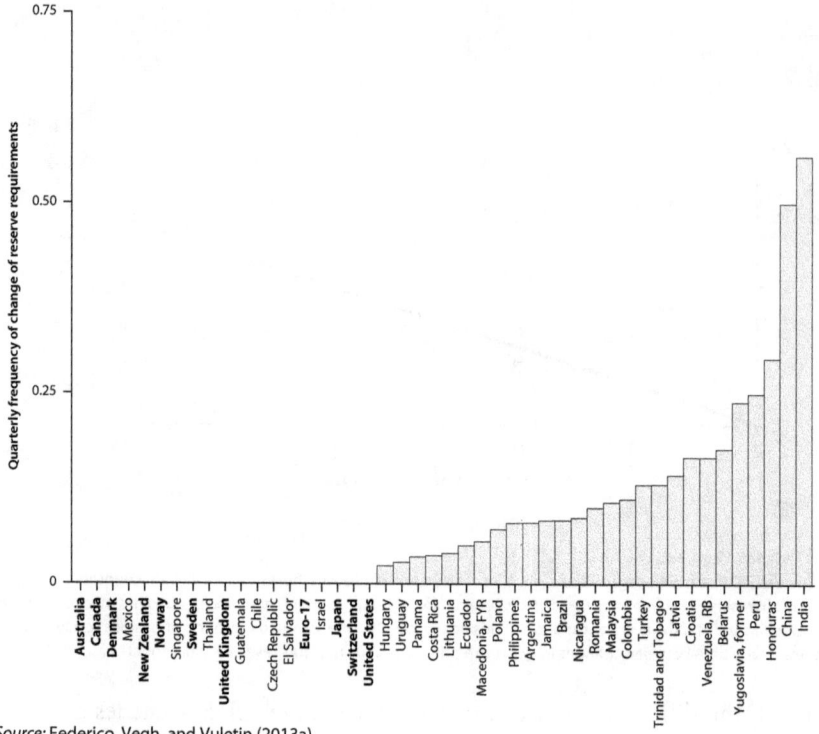

Source: Federico, Vegh, and Vuletin (2013a).

Figure 2.4 Cyclicality of Reserve Requirement Policy (1970–2011)

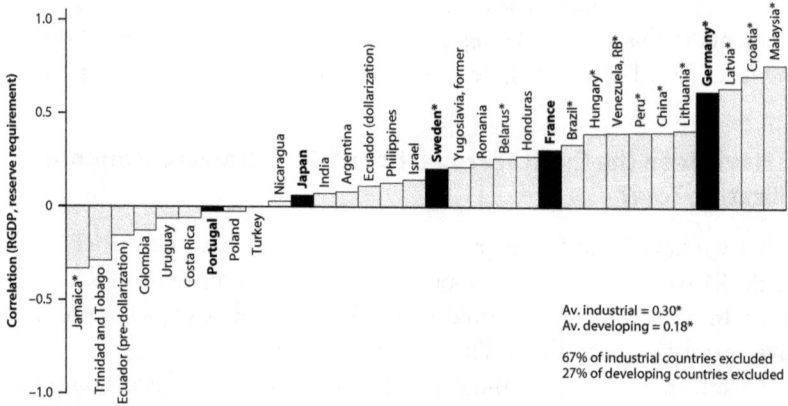

Source: Federico, Vegh, and Vuletin (2013a).
Note: Average reserve requirement is used for calculations. Sample only includes active reserve requirement policy countries.
* indicates that the correlation is statistical significance at 5 percent level.

Figure 2.5a Cyclicality of Reserve Requirement Policy (1970–2004)

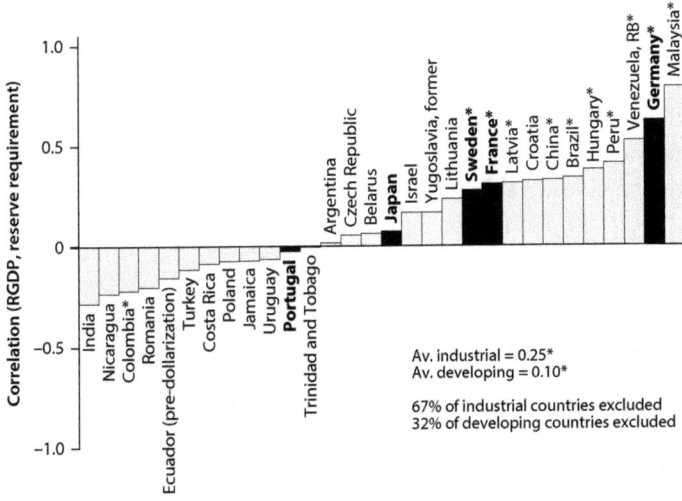

Av. industrial = 0.25*
Av. developing = 0.10*

67% of industrial countries excluded
32% of developing countries excluded

Source: Federico, Vegh, and Vuletin (2013a).
Note: Average reserve requirement is used for calculations. Sample only includes active reserve requirement policy countries. RGDP indicates real gross domestic product.
* indicates that the correlation is statistical significance at 5 percent level.

Figure 2.5b Cyclicality of Reserve Requirement Policy (2005–11)

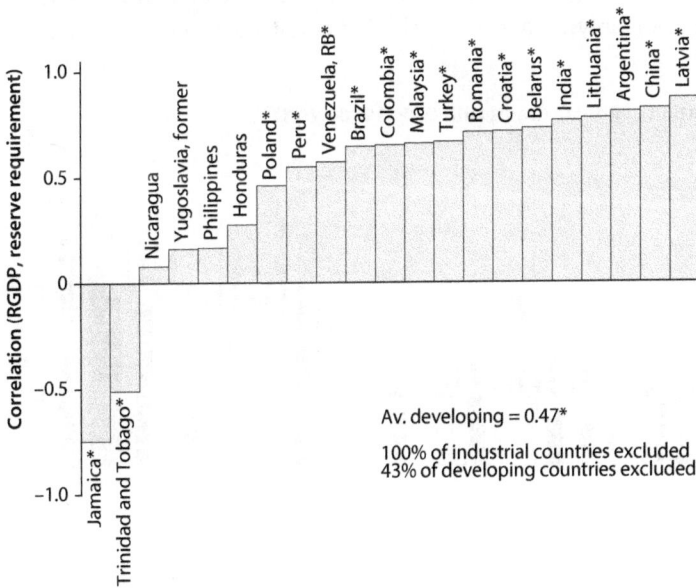

Av. developing = 0.47*

100% of industrial countries excluded
43% of developing countries excluded

Source: Federico, Vegh, and Vuletin (2013a).
Note: Average reserve requirement is used for calculations. Sample only includes active reserve requirement policy countries.
* indicates that the correlation is statistical significance at 5 percent level.

number of active countries with countercyclical RRP was 60 percent (or 18 out of 30) but after 2004 the number rises sharply to 90 percent (or 19 out of 21). Particularly striking is the fact that in the post-2004 period, there is not a single industrial country that has pursued active RRP.

The evidence thus suggests that (i) reserve requirements have been used fairly frequently as a macroeconomic stabilization tool (that is, countercyclically); (ii) their use has increased considerable since 2004, which is consistent with anecdotal evidence to this effect; and (iii) no industrial country has used RRP actively in the post-2004 period.

How Is RRP Related to the Credit Cycle?

How is RRP related to the credit cycle? After all, we would think that the channel through which reserve requirements may smooth out the real GDP cycle is by dampening the amplitude of the real credit cycle. In this respect, the first observation is that, as expected and illustrated in figure 2.6, real credit is highly procyclical in both industrial and developing countries. Hence, the procyclicality of credit *per se* cannot offer an explanation as to why some countries actively use RRP while others do not. In line with this, our policy rationale offered below relies instead on the behavior of the nominal exchange rate over the business cycle.

We do find in the data, however, a relationship between the *level* of the credit to GDP ratio and the use of RR.[6] Specifically, figure 2.7 shows that the credit to GDP ratio is considerably higher in developing countries making active use of

Figure 2.6 Correlation of Private Credit with GDP (1970–2011)

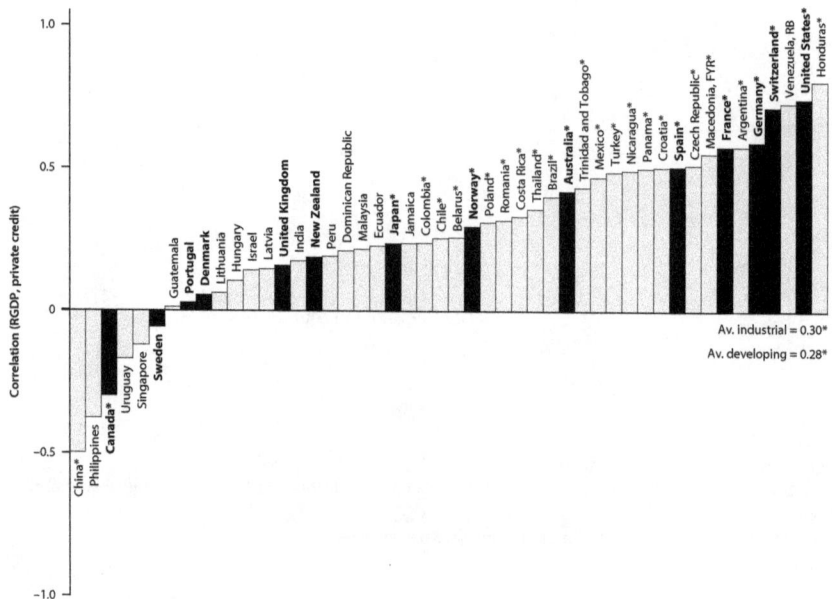

Source: Federico, Vegh, and Vuletin (2013a).
Note: * indicates statistical significance at the 5 percent level.

Figure 2.7 Private Credit for Developing Countries (1970–2011)

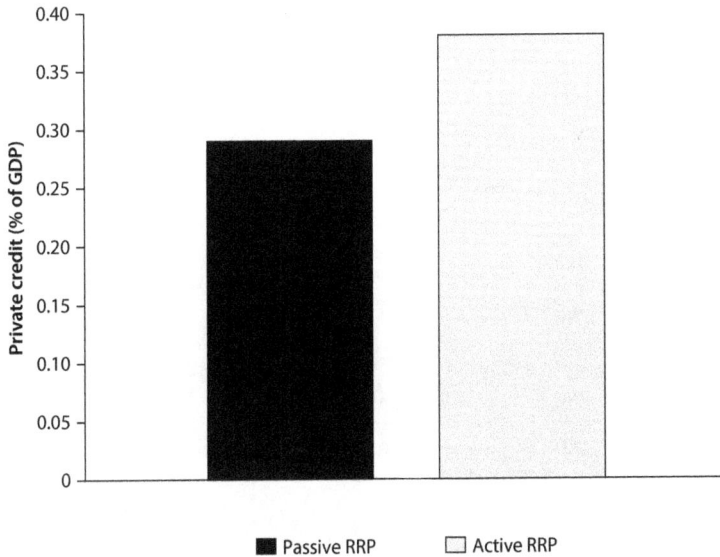

Source: Federico, Vegh, and Vuletin (2013a).
Note: GDP indicates gross domestic product; RRP indicates reserve requirement policy.

RRP (38 percent) compared to developing countries that do not (29 percent).[7] Even more telling, figure 2.8 shows that, for active countries, the correlation between RR and the cycle (a measure of the intensity of RRP as a macroeconomic stabilization tool) is an increasing function of the level of credit to GDP. In other words, the higher is the level of credit in the economy, the more countercyclical is the use of RR.[8] This might reflect the fact that emerging economies with higher levels of credit (relative to GDP) tend to have more pronounced fluctuations triggered by the capital flows cycle, as analyzed below.

What Is the Relation between RRP and Monetary Policy?

The fact that, since 2004, 90 percent of active developing countries have pursued countercyclical RRP is remarkable when contrasted with the countercyclical use of the interest rate, clearly the most ubiquitous and flexible policy tool. Indeed, as illustrated in figure 2.9, while all industrial countries (black bars) exhibit a positive correlation between the cyclical components of the policy rate and real GDP (indicating countercyclical monetary policy), only 59 percent (or 22 out of 37) of developing countries do so. In terms of correlations significantly different from zero, the figure for industrial countries is 73 percent (or 11 out of 15) compared to 27 percent (or 10 out of 37) for developing countries. In fact, the average correlation for industrial countries is 0.40 (and significantly different from zero), compared to 0.07 (and not significantly different from zero) for emerging countries. In other words, the average industrial country pursues countercyclical monetary policy, whereas the average emerging country is acyclical.

Reserve Requirements in the Brave New Macroprudential World
http://dx.doi.org/10.1596/978-1-4648-0212-6

Figure 2.8 Cyclicality of RRP versus Private Credit (Active Countries, 1970–2011)

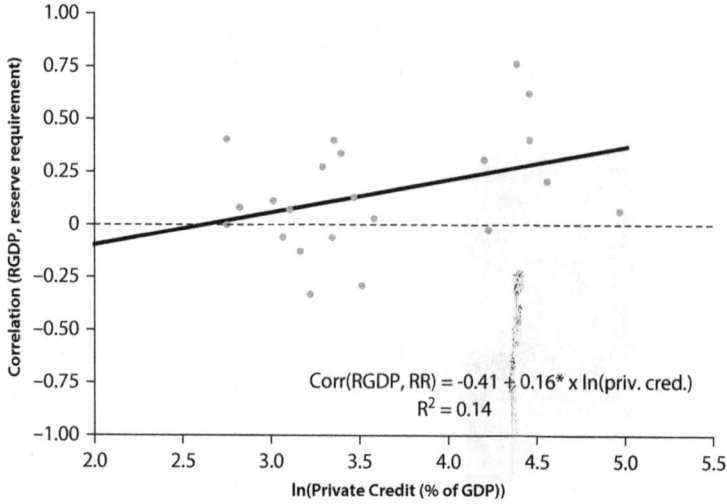

$$\text{Corr(RGDP, RR)} = -0.41 + 0.16^* \times \ln(\text{priv. cred.})$$
$$R^2 = 0.14$$

Source: Federico, Vegh, and Vuletin (2013a).
Note: * indicates statistical significance at the 5 percent level.

Figure 2.9 Cyclicality of Interest Rate Policy (1970–2011)

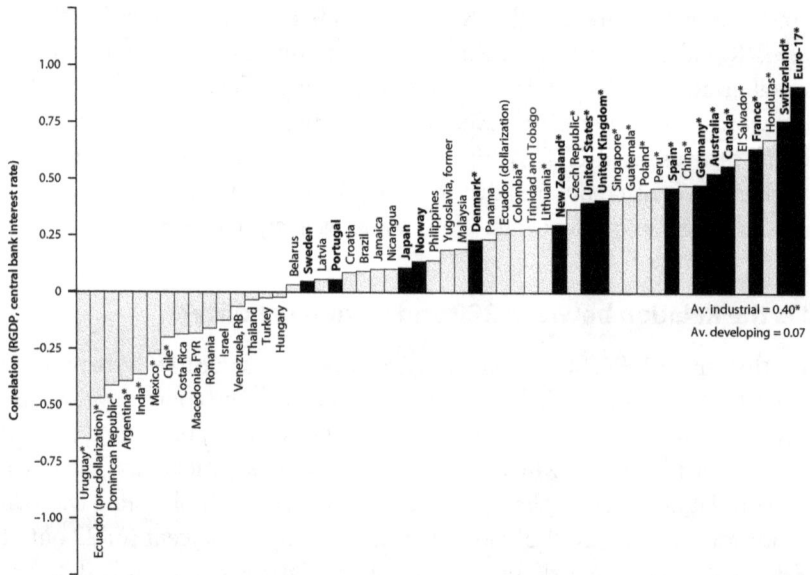

Av. industrial = 0.40*
Av. developing = 0.07

Source: Federico, Vegh, and Vuletin (2013a).
Note: * indicates statistical significance at the 5 percent level.

Again, the averages over such a long period of time (1970–2011) mask some important changes. As analyzed in detail in Vegh and Vuletin (2013), in the last decade or so we have observed a process of "graduation" whereby many developing countries have switched from procyclical to countercyclical monetary policy. In terms of our sample, we see that for the pre-2004 period just 16 percent (or 6 out of 37) of developing countries exhibit a positive (and significantly different from zero) correlation, as illustrated in figure 2.10, Panel a. The corresponding figure increases to 41 percent (or 15 out of 37) for the post-2004 period (figure 2.10, Panel b). In fact, we can see that the average correlation for developing countries increases from 0.07 (and not significantly different from zero) to 0.27 (and significantly different from zero). As argued below, this graduation process can be explained by a fall in the fear of free falling (that is, a reduction in the need to defend the currency in bad times).

How are RRP and monetary policy related over the business cycle? To answer this question, we constructed a "policy mix matrix" (table 2.1) that classifies countries according to the cyclical properties of RRP and monetary policy. Since countries may be procyclical, acyclical, or countercyclical, there are nine possible cells. Notice that most industrial countries are on the second row because most of them are acyclical when it comes to RRP (that is, they do not use RRP for macroeconomic stabilization purposes). In fact, most industrial countries (11 out of 15 or 73 percent) fall in the [2,3] cell, colored orange, given that their monetary policy is countercyclical.

Figure 2.10a Cyclicality of Interest Rate Policy (1970–2004)

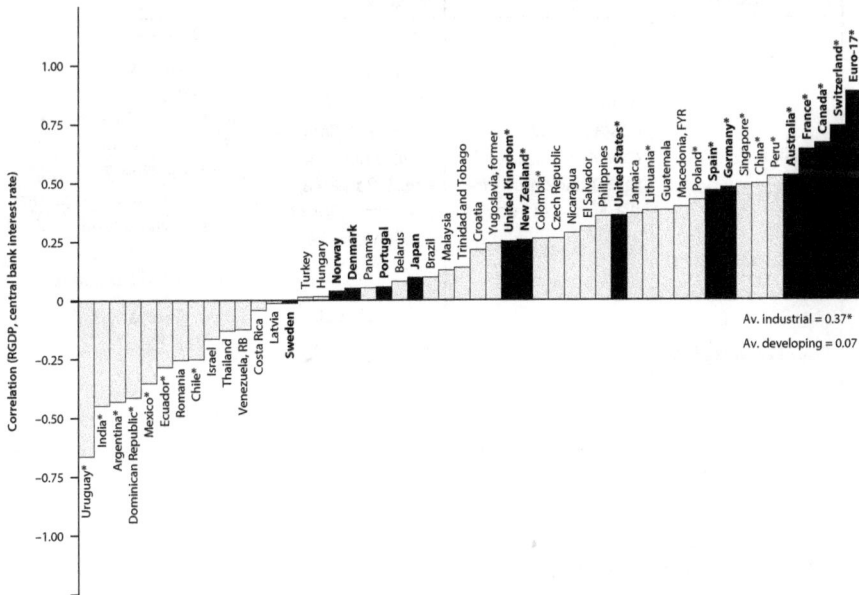

Source: Federico, Vegh, and Vuletin (2013a).
Note: * indicates statistical significance at the 5 percent level.

Figure 2.10b Cyclicality of Interest Rate Policy (2005–11)

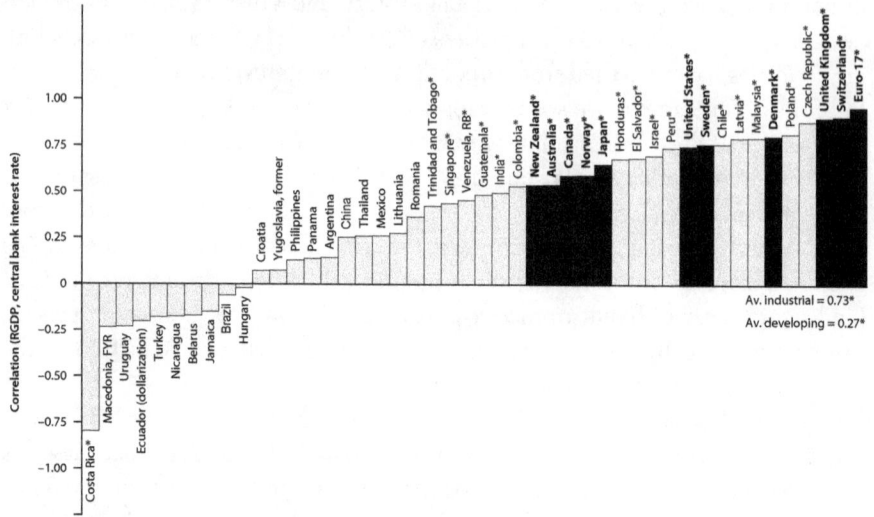

Source: Federico, Vegh, and Vuletin (2013a).
Note: * indicates statistical significance at the 5 percent level.

Table 2.1 Policy Mix Matrix (1970–2011)

		Central bank interest rate policy		
		Procyclical (1)	**Acyclical (2)**	**Countercyclical (3)**
Reserve requirement policy	**Procyclical (1)**		Jamaica	
	Acyclical (2)	Argentina, Chile, Costa Rica, Dominican Republic, Ecuador (predollarization), India, Mexico, Uruguay	Israel, **Japan**, Macedonia, FYR, Nicaragua, Panama, Philippines, **Portugal**, Romania, Yugoslavia, former, Thailand, Turkey	**Australia, Canada,** Colombia, Czech Republic, **Denmark,** Ecuador (dollarization), El Salvador, **Euro-17, France,** Guatemala, Honduras, **New Zealand, Norway,** Poland, Singapore, **Spain, Switzerland,** Trinidad and Tobago, **United Kingdom, United States**
	Countercyclical (3)		Belarus, Brazil, Croatia, Hungary, Latvia, **Sweden**, Venezuela, RB	China, **Germany**, Lithuania, Malaysia, Peru
		Substitutes		Complements

Source: Federico, Vegh, and Vuletin (2013a).

In contrast, 10 developing countries (or 27 percent of all developing countries in our sample) fall in the third row because they exhibit countercyclical RRP. Of these 10 developing countries, 6 fall in the cell [3,2], given that they have had acyclical monetary policy, while the remaining 4 fall in cell [3,3] because they have had countercyclical monetary policy.

As a matter of definition, we will refer to countries falling in cell [3,3] as using RRP as a *complement* to monetary policy in the sense that both policies reinforce each other.[9] These are cases in which both RRP and monetary policy are countercyclical, so that in good (bad) times both RR and the policy interest rate are increased (lowered). In contrast, countries that fall in cell [3,2] and, potentially, cell [3,1] are cases in which RRP acts as a *substitute* for interest rate policy because reserve requirements perform the function that the interest rate cannot due to the need of either defending the currency in bad times or not attracting more capital inflows in good times.

Further, we interpret cell [2,1] as a "bad place" to be because here countries feel compelled to use monetary policy procyclically (for reasons to be discussed below) but are not taking advantage of RR as a second instrument. On the other hand, we can view [2,3] as the "promised land," in terms of policy making. The reason is that here countries can use monetary policy for countercyclical purposes without fearing the effects of countercyclical interest rates on the exchange rate and/or capital inflows, presumably reflecting a large degree of policy and institutional credibility.[10]

As before, we break the sample into before and after 2004 and construct the policy matrices for each period, as illustrated in table 2.2. Comparing the pre- and post-2004 policy mix matrices in tables 2.2, Panels a and b, three important changes are worth noting: (i) the number of developing countries pursuing procyclical interest rate policy falls from seven in the early period to just one in the more recent period; (ii) the number of developing countries engaging in countercyclical RRP increases from 7 to 15, and (iii) developing countries using monetary policy and RRP as substitutes (as captured in cell [2,2]) increases from 5 to 8, whereas developing countries using monetary policy and RRP as complements (as captured in cell [3,3]) increases from 2 to 7.

In this context, one can imagine different "routes" that countries may take in the policy journey from cell [2,1], a "bad place to be," to cell [2,3], the "promised land." One route would be the "direct route" that Chile took. Notice that Chile went from cell [2,1] in the pre-2005 period to cell [2,3] in the post-2004 period. This is remarkable because, in our view, it can only happen in the context of a notable improvement in policy/institutional credibility, as discussed below. In such a case, a country like Chile may not need to resort to countercyclical RRP, which is presumably the situation of a typical industrial country.[11]

A more common route (involving several stages) would be to go from cell [2,1] to cell [3,2], then to cell [3,3], and finally to cell [2,3]. One could even add an additional stage in which countries would go from cell [2,1] to cell [2,2] and only then to cell [3,2]. Mexico and Uruguay, for instance, have gone from cell [2,1] in the pre-2005 period to cell [2,2] in the post-2004 period. This is presumably an improvement in the policy mix because they have graduated from monetary policy procyclicality, but the fact that they are in cell [2,2] implies that they have no countercyclical tool.[12] In principle, they would benefit from moving to cell [3,2] where they would be using RR as a countercyclical tool.

Reserve Requirements in the Brave New Macroprudential World
http://dx.doi.org/10.1596/978-1-4648-0212-6

Table 2.2a Policy Mix Matrix (1970–2004)

		Central bank interest rate policy		
		Procyclical (1)	*Acyclical (2)*	*Countercyclical (3)*
Reserve requirement policy	**Procyclical (1)**			Colombia
	Acyclical (2)	Argentina, Chile, Dominican Republic, Ecuador, India, Mexico, Uruguay	Belarus, Costa Rica, Croatia, Czech Republic, Denmark, El Salvador, Guatemala, Israel, Jamaica, Japan, Macedonia, FYR, Nicaragua, Norway, Panama, Philippines, Portugal, Romania, Yugoslavia, former, Thailand, Trinidad and Tobago, Turkey	**Australia, Canada, Euro-17,** Lithuania, **New Zealand,** Poland, Singapore, **Spain, Switzerland, United Kingdom, United States,**
	Countercyclical (3)		Brazil, Hungary, Latvia, Malaysia, **Sweden,** Venezuela, RB	China, **France, Germany,** Peru,

Substitutes   Complements

Source: Federico, Vegh, and Vuletin (2013a).

Table 2.2b Policy Mix Matrix (2005–11)

		Central bank interest rate policy		
		Procyclical (1)	*Acyclical (2)*	*Countercyclical (3)*
Reserve requirement policy	**Procyclical (1)**		Jamaica	Trinidad and Tobago
	Acyclical (2)	Costa Rica	Ecuador (dollarization), Hungary, Macedonia, FYR, Mexico, Nicaragua, Panama, Philippines, Yugoslavia, former, Thailand, Uruguay,	**Australia, Canada,** Chile, Czech Republic, **Denmark,** El Salvador, **Euro-17,** Guatemala, Honduras, Israel, **Japan, New Zealand, Norway,** Singapore, **Sweden, Switzerland, United Kingdom, United States**
	Countercyclical (3)		Argentina, Belarus, Brazil, China, Croatia, Lithuania, Romania, Turkey	Colombia, India, Latvia, Malaysia, Peru, Poland, Venezuela, RB

Substitutes   Complements

Source: Federico, Vegh, and Vuletin (2013a).

How Does Foreign Exchange Market Intervention Fit into the Picture?

As is well known, developing countries often intervene in foreign exchange markets, buying (selling) foreign currency in good (bad) times to prevent an appreciation (depreciation) of the domestic currency. The extent of foreign exchange market intervention, however, will depend on the particular exchange rate regime/policy mix that policy makers choose in order to deal with the capital flow cycle. Clearly, under a fixed or predetermined exchange rate regime, foreign exchange market intervention will be geared towards maintaining a particular value of the exchange rate while the monetary policy should play a minor role, if any.[13] Under a relatively clean floating exchange rate, foreign exchange market intervention would be minimal with monetary policy playing a much larger role. The role of RRP under different exchange rate regimes has been much less studied both theoretically and empirically. In any event—and since over long periods of time, the exchange rate regime is a policy choice—we would like to let the data speak and tell us the extent of foreign exchange market intervention and how it relates to both monetary policy and RRP.

Figure 2.11 plots the correlation between (the cyclical components of) international reserves and real GDP for our sample. It turns out that 54 percent (or 20 out of 37) of developing countries exhibit a positive (and significantly different from zero) correlation, clearly suggesting a considerable degree of foreign exchange market intervention.[14] The corresponding figure for industrial countries is 38 (or 5 out of 13). In terms of the before and after (not shown), the figure for developing countries has increased from 33 percent (or 11 out of 33 countries) to 48 percent (or 16 out of 33).

How are monetary policy and foreign exchange market intervention related? In order to investigate this, figure 2.12 plots the correlation between (the cyclical components of) international reserves and real GDP on the vertical axis against the correlation between (the cyclical components of) the policy interest rate and real GDP. We can see that the regression line is negatively sloped (and significantly so). This means that countries that pursue a procyclical monetary policy (that is, have a negative correlation between the policy rate and the business cycle) intervene more heavily in foreign exchange markets. As discussed

Figure 2.11 Cyclicality of International Reserves (1970–2011)

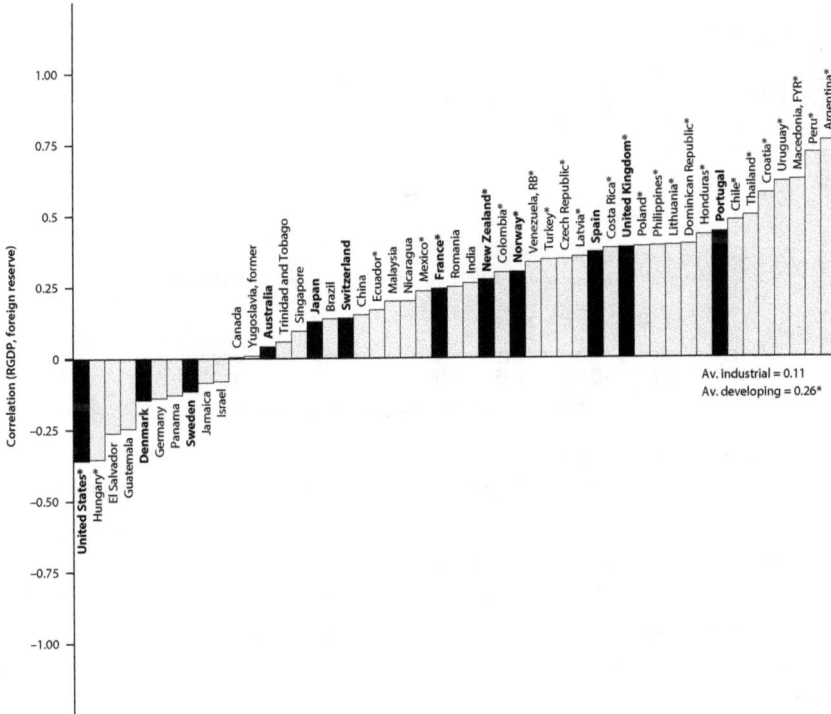

Source: Federico, Vegh, and Vuletin (2013a).
Note: * indicates statistical significance at the 5 percent level.

Reserve Requirements in the Brave New Macroprudential World
http://dx.doi.org/10.1596/978-1-4648-0212-6

Figure 2.12 Monetary versus Foreign Exchange Market Intervention Policy (1970–2011)

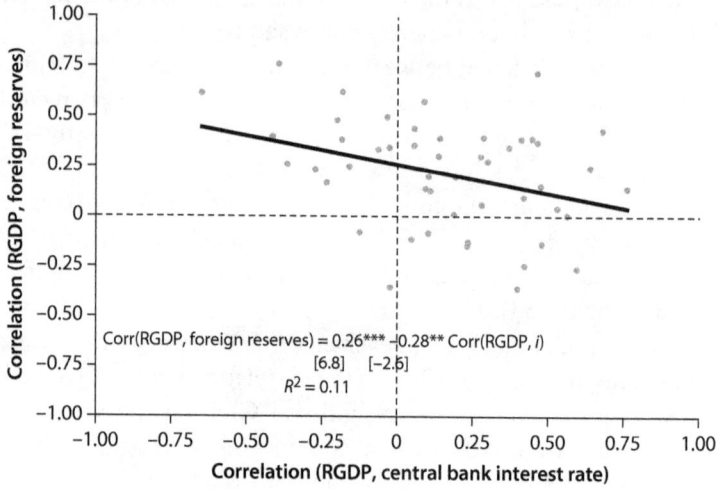

Corr(RGDP, foreign reserves) = 0.26*** −0.28** Corr(RGDP, i)
[6.8]   [−2.5]
R^2 = 0.11

Source: Federico, Vegh, and Vuletin (2013a).
Note: *, **, and *** indicate statistical significance at the 10 percent, 5 percent, and 1 percent levels, respectively.

Figure 2.13 RRP versus Foreign Exchange Market Intervention (1970–2011)

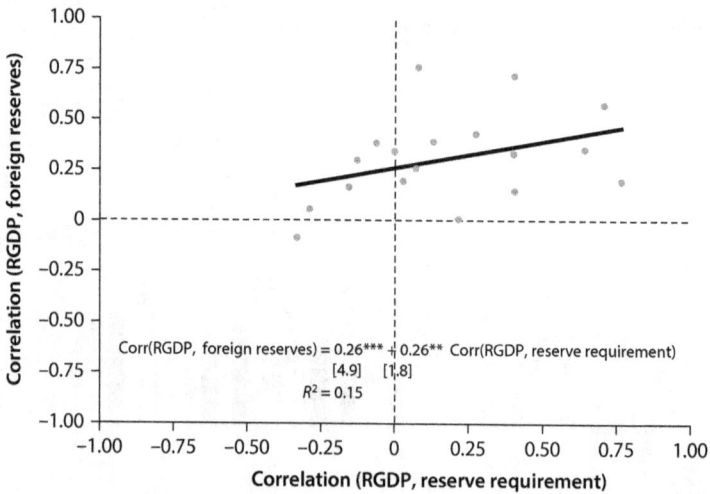

Corr(RGDP, foreign reserves) = 0.26*** + 0.26** Corr(RGDP, reserve requirement)
[4.9]   [1.8]
R^2 = 0.15

Source: Federico, Vegh, and Vuletin (2013a).
Note: *, **, and *** indicate statistical significance at the 10 percent, 5 percent, and 1 percent levels, respectively.

below, such a pattern would be consistent with the idea that developing countries might feel the need to defend their currencies in bad times by both raising interest rates and selling foreign assets and that they need to fight appreciation in good times by buying foreign assets and lowering (or at least not raising) interest rates.

How are RRP and foreign exchange market intervention related? Figure 2.13 plots the correlation between (the cyclical components of) international reserves and real GDP on the vertical axis against the correlation between (the cyclical components of) reserve requirements and real GDP on the horizontal axis. The corresponding regression line is positive (and significantly so). This implies that countries that pursue a countercyclical RRP tend to intervene more heavily in foreign exchange markets. Hence, the picture that emerges is one where developing countries concerned about currency depreciation in bad times raise interest rates and intervene in foreign exchange markets to prevent further depreciation, yet at the same time lower reserve requirements in an attempt to stimulate credit expansion and, hence, economic activity.

Notes

1. Formally—and to account for the high variability of the business cycle duration within countries—we will classify a country as pursuing an active RRP if the average duration between changes in RR is lower than the average duration of the business cycle plus one standard deviation.

2. It is, of course, possible that reserve requirements are being changed for reasons other than smoothing out the business cycle (that is, for microprudential reasons). Casual observation, however, suggests that the frequency of changes for microprudential purposes is much lower.

3. Countries with zero frequency of change would have an "infinite" amount of time between changes and are plotted out of scale. We say "generally" because, to keep it simple, the scatter plot does not allow for the one standard deviation of the business cycle duration embedded in our formal definition above. In the figure, a dot (cross) denotes an active (passive) country.

4. Of the 15 industrial countries in this subsample, 8 have in fact no legal reserve requirement.

5. By definition, countercyclical (procyclical) RRP refers to a situation in which the correlation between RR and the business cycle is positive (negative). Naturally, the idea of countercyclical RRP would be to cool down the economy in good times by raising RR and to stimulate output in bad times by lowering RR.

6. Not surprisingly—given that credit is highly procyclical in almost every country—we do not find a positive correlation between RRP and the ratio of the variance of credit to the variance of GDP. But neither do we find a positive relation between RRP and the variance of credit (the coefficient is not significantly different from zero). The problem here could be one of reverse causality since an effective RRP should reduce the variance of credit and thus possibly offset the positive correlation that one may have expected. To dig deeper into this issue, we would need to find valid instruments for the variance of credit.

7. This difference is significant at the 1 percent level.

8. This relation continues to hold even if we control for the level of GDP per capita, suggesting that what matters is the credit to GDP ratio regardless of the level of development of the economy.

9. Notice that this definition of complements and substitutes only focuses on the comovement of the two policy instruments and thus should not be confused with the game theoretical concepts of strategic complementarity and substitutability à la Bulow, Geanakoplos, and Klemperer (1985).

Reserve Requirements in the Brave New Macroprudential World
http://dx.doi.org/10.1596/978-1-4648-0212-6

10. Vegh and Vuletin (2013) formally link graduation from monetary procyclicality to institutional improvement. Of course, countries may still want to use RR as systemic risk-driven macroprudential policy. In theory, as well, countries might want to use both monetary policy and RR countercyclically if they feel that the monetary transmission channel of monetary policy is not strong enough. Revealed preference, however, suggests that this is not the case and that industrial countries (many of which in fact do not even have legal RR) do not feel the need to supplement monetary policy with RR. Hence, our label of "promised land" is meant to convey an observed state of affairs rather than an optimal prescription regarding the mix of monetary policy and RR in mature countries. In fact, this is clearly an area that warrants further analytical work.

11. This would be a "one-step" graduation process, which is the one (implicitly) highlighted by Vegh, and Vuletin (2013) for the case of monetary policy and Frankel, Vegh, and Vuletin (2013) for the case of fiscal policy. For a more detailed analysis of institutional changes that may have allowed Chile to graduate, see Frankel (2011).

12. Not even fiscal policy because, according to Frankel, Vegh, and Vuletin (2013), both Mexico and Uruguay continue to be procyclical even in the more recent period.

13. Of course, under perfect capital mobility, there is no role for monetary policy. Under imperfect capital mobility, there may be a role for monetary policy even under fixed exchange rates; see Lahiri and Vegh (2003) and Flood and Jeanne (2005) for models along these lines.

14. Of course, foreign exchange market intervention is automatic under any predetermined exchange rates regime and the higher correlation could reflect a preponderance of such regimes in emerging markets. This, however, is irrelevant for our point because the exchange rate regime is itself a policy choice and hence must reflect the policy makers' preferences in terms of how much the nominal exchange rate is allowed to fluctuate.

CHAPTER 3

An Illustration of Policy Responses for Four Latin American Countries

To further illustrate the policy mix that developing countries may typically use in response to different shocks, we estimated an econometric model for four Latin American countries (Argentina, Brazil, Colombia, and Uruguay) and simulated the policy response to a shock to gross domestic product (GDP) and a shock to the rate of depreciation. Technically, we estimated a panel vector-autoregression model and used a narrative approach to distinguish between exogenous (to the business cycle) and endogenous changes in reserve requirements. Box 3.1 describes in great detail the identification strategy used for the identification of endogenous and exogenous changes in reserve requirements.[1]

Figure 3.1 illustrates the policy response to an increase in real GDP. We can see that while the policy rate is lowered (Panel A), both reserve requirements (Panel B) and international reserves (Panel C) increase.[2]

To interpret such policy mix, think of a recession (a fall in real GDP). Then, figure 3.1 indicates that policy makers would increase the policy rate (to defend the currency), lower reserve requirements (to stimulate the economy), and sell foreign exchange (also to defend the currency). This is fully consistent with the results obtained for the whole sample above that suggested that monetary policy and reserve requirement policies (RRP) have acted as substitutes while RRP and foreign exchange market intervention have been complements.

Figure 3.2 captures the response of the three policy instruments to an increase in the rate of depreciation. The policy rate increases (Panel A), there is no significant change in reserve requirements (RR) (Panel B), and international reserves fall (Panel C). This policy response is entirely consistent with the idea that, when faced with a depreciating currency, policy makers in emerging markets increase interest rates and sell foreign assets to try to stabilize the value of the currency.

Figure 3.1 Policy Response to a Real GDP Shock (One Standard-Deviation Shock)
The solid lines represent the response of each variable to a shock. Dashed lines represent
95% error bands.

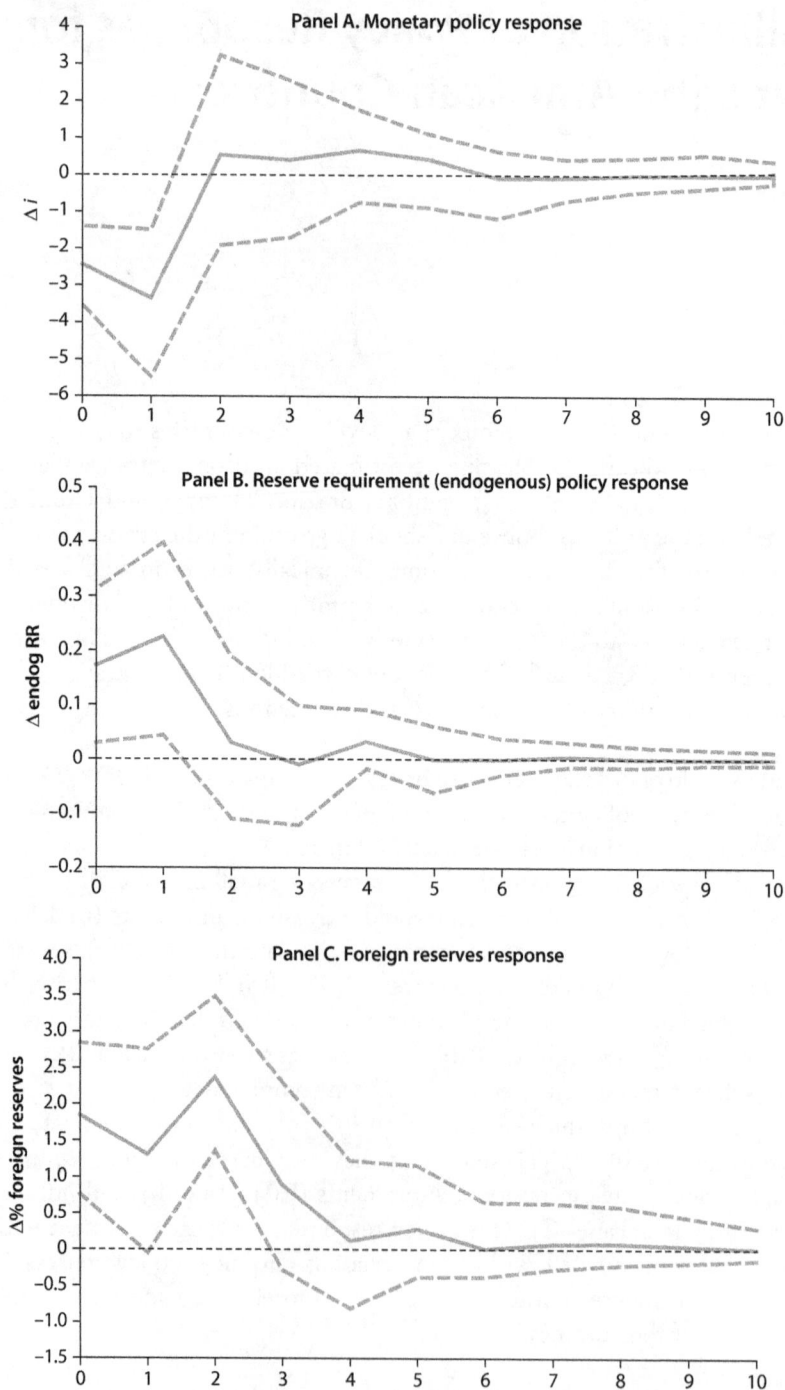

Panel A. Monetary policy response

Panel B. Reserve requirement (endogenous) policy response

Panel C. Foreign reserves response

Source: Federico, Vegh, and Vuletin (2013b).

Figure 3.2 Policy Response to a Nominal Exchange Rate Depreciation Shock
The solid lines represent the response of each variable to a shock. Dashed lines represent
95% error bands.

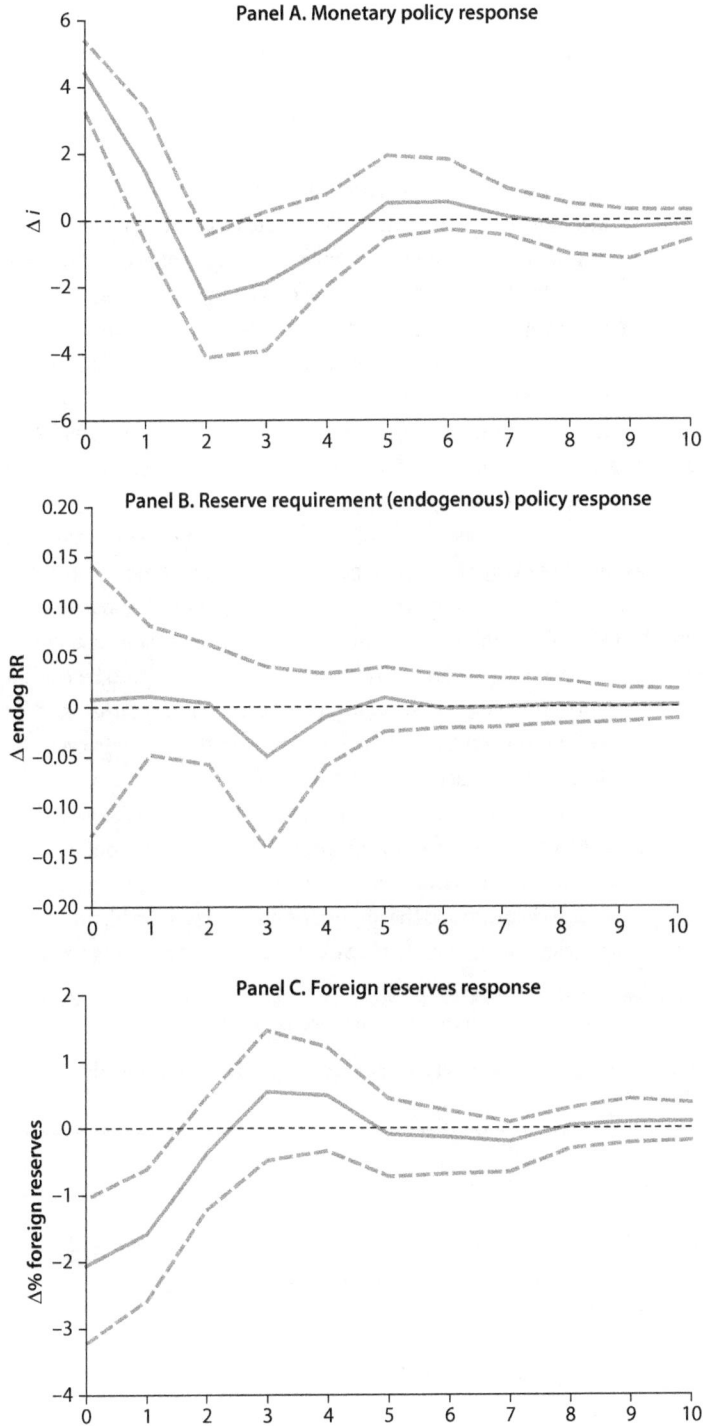

Panel A. Monetary policy response

Panel B. Reserve requirement (endogenous) policy response

Panel C. Foreign reserves response

Source: Federico, Vegh, and Vuletin (2013b).

Reserve Requirements in the Brave New Macroprudential World
http://dx.doi.org/10.1596/978-1-4648-0212-6

Box 3.1   The Narrative Approach to Identification

Following Blanchard and Perotti (2002), the traditional strategy used to identify fiscal, mone-tary, and (more recently) reserve requirement shocks has relied on vector autoregression analysis (VAR) together with timing assumptions regarding the dynamics between policy and output. On the fiscal side—using quarterly data—it has been assumed that government spending requires at least one quarter to respond to news about the state of the economy and that active fiscal policy may affect output in the same quarter (that is, government spend-ing is more "exogenous" or slow moving than output). The opposite has been assumed on the monetary front (using monthly data). While changes in policy rates are not allowed to have contemporaneous (that is, within the month) effects on macroeconomic variables, develop-ments in the stance of the economy are allowed to affect monetary policy. Mimicking this monetary identification strategy, several recent papers (for example, Glocker and Towbin, 2012; Tovar, Garcia-Escribano, and Vera Martin, 2012) have analyzed the impact of reserve requirement changes on credit and economic activity obtaining—in some circumstances—some puzzling results. For example, Tovar, Garcia-Escribano, and Vera Martin (2012) find that an increase in reserve requirements increases private credit.

Federico, Vegh, and Vuletin (2013b), rely on the use of Romer-Romer-type narratives to identify shocks to reserve requirements.[a] To the best of our knowledge, this is the first instance in this literature in which such an approach has been followed. Using historical documents, including International Monetary Fund (IMF) and central banks reports, we classify changes in reserve requirements into (i) endogenous changes, which were mainly motivated by current or projected output fluctuations (that is, when output growth differs from normal) and (ii) exogenous changes, which were triggered by reasons exogenous to the business cycle, in-cluding microprudential factors and financial liberalization. When we then incorporate the exogenous changes in reserve requirements into our VAR analysis, we find that, as expected, higher reserve requirements reduce private credit and output.[b] Our analysis also confirms that endogenous changes in reserve requirements, in turn, respond positively and strongly to out-put shocks. This striking difference clearly shows the importance of following an identification strategy that is able to isolate policy innovations that are exogenous to the business cycle.

a. See, for example, Romer and Romer (2010) and Riera-Crichton, Vegh, and Vuletin (2012) for a discussion of the use of narratives to evaluate the effect of taxation policy, and Romer and Romer (2004) and Coibion (2012) for the case of monetary policy.
b. Moreover, past output fluctuations are poor predictors of changes in exogenous reserve requirements changes, sup-porting our narrative categorization.

Notes

1. The analysis covers the period 1995–2010 for Brazil and 1992–2011 for Argentina, Colombia, and Uruguay. Since our sample period covers Argentina's Convertibility plan—and to test the robustness of our results—we estimated all panel VAR regres-sions excluding each country one-at-a-time and obtained the same results. For details, see the background paper by Federico, Vegh, and Vuletin (2013b).

2. We broke the sample into positive and negative increases to GDP and results were the same.

CHAPTER 4

Policy Rationale

The previous chapter has illustrated the fact that developing countries tend to pursue an active reserve requirement policy (RRP) when they are pursuing an either acyclical or procyclical monetary policy. This suggests that these countries may have been unable to lower (increase) interest rates in bad (good) times for fear of letting their currency depreciate (appreciate) too fast. In other words, these countries may have resorted to reserve requirements as a second policy instrument in their quest to hit two different targets: real gross domestic product (GDP) and the exchange rate. This chapter develops this argument and examines the country characteristics that may affect the choice of such a policy mix.

The Need for a Second Instrument

In our view of the world, the critical feature of emerging markets' business cycle that may trigger the need for a second policy instrument is the fact that there is a negative correlation between (the cyclical components of) the nominal exchange rate and real GDP.[1] This is illustrated in figure 4.1 where we can see that 89 percent of developing countries (that is, 33 out of 37) exhibit a negative correlation. By and large, then, the typical business cycle in an emerging country entails an exchange rate that is below (above) trend in good (bad) times. In other words, in good (bad) times the currency is relatively appreciated (depreciated). Further, the depreciation of the currency in bad times is often sharp and triggers large capital outflows which, in turn, exacerbate the currency depreciation leading to a vicious spiral of capital outflows, depreciation, and recession. More often than not, policy makers feel that they have little choice but to defend the currency because if the currency collapses so does the macroeconomy.[2] The need to defend the domestic currency in bad times is best exemplified by International Monetary Fund (IMF) policy advice during the 1997 Asian crisis.[3]

Figure 4.1 Cyclicality of Nominal Exchange Rates (1970–2011)

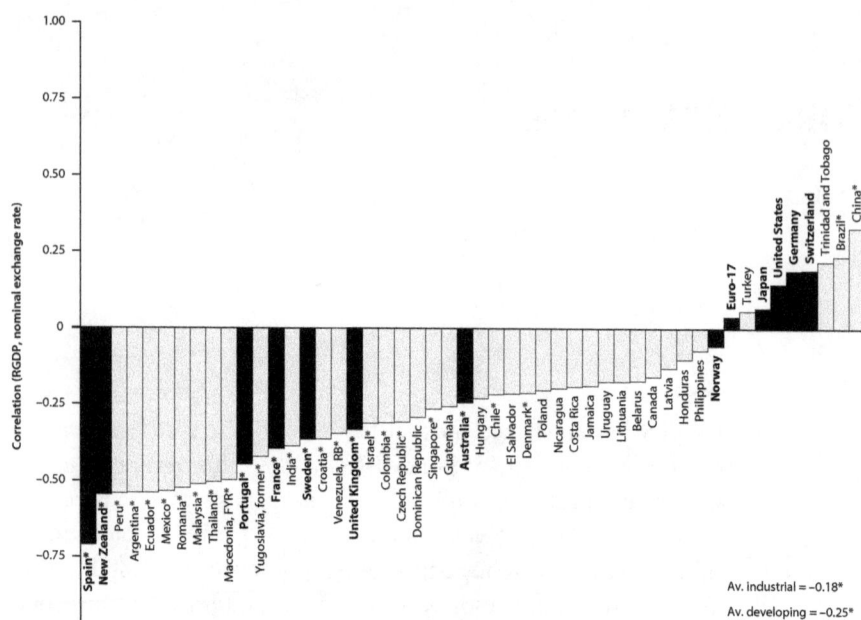

Source: Cordella and Gupta (2014).
Note: * indicates statistical significance at the 5 percent level.

Figure 4.2 illustrates the defense of the currency in bad times by plotting along the horizontal axis the correlation between the nominal exchange rate and GDP and along the vertical axis the correlation between monetary policy and GDP. We can see that the regression line is significantly positive suggesting that the more the currency depreciates in bad times (that is, the more to the left we are along the horizontal axis), the more procyclical monetary policy is (that is, the more pronounced is the interest rate defense of the currency).

The need to increase interest rates during bad times (or at least not lower them) presents a dilemma for emerging market policy makers because, in and of itself, higher interest rates will only exacerbate the fall in output. The opposite situation (good times) presents an analogous dilemma: in good times—when capital is flowing in, the currency is appreciating, the economy is overheating, and inflation is going up—a countercyclical monetary policy of higher interest rates to cool down the economy will only exacerbate capital inflows and currency appreciation because it makes domestic-currency assets more attractive for foreign investors. This "fear of capital inflows" may induce policy makers not to raise interest rates in good times and use higher reserve requirements to cool down the economy.

In contrast, industrial countries are typically much less concerned with exchange rate fluctuations either because (i) the exchange rate correlates positively with the business cycle (as is the case for the Euro-area, Japan, the United States, and Germany in figure 4.1) or, (ii) if the exchange rate does correlate

Figure 4.2 Monetary versus "Currency Defense" Policy (1970–2011)

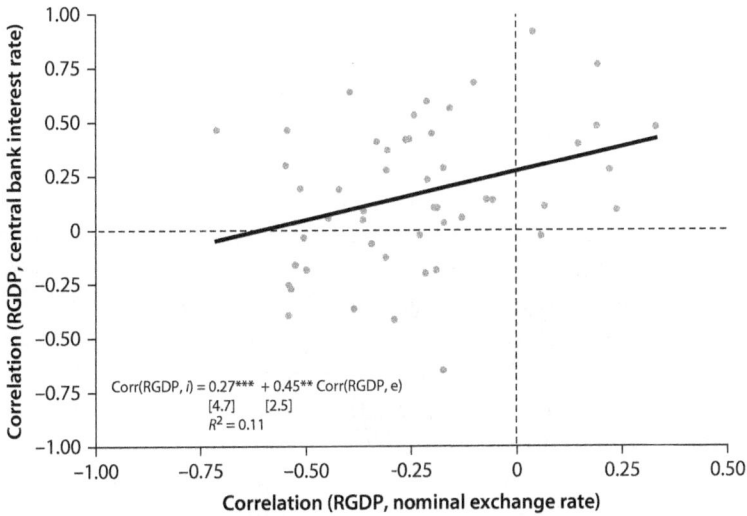

Source: Federico, Vegh, and Vuletin (2013a).
Note: *, **, and *** indicate statistical significance at the 10 percent, 5 percent, and 1 percent levels, respectively.

negatively, it is no cause for concern. In other words, even if the currency depreciates in bad times in an industrial country, markets would not interpret this as a
signal that policy makers are losing control of the macroeconomy and/or that
capital outflows will accelerate. In the United States, for example, fluctuations in
the value of the dollar have normally little direct impact on Fed's policy.

The need for a second instrument may, of course, be thought of in terms of
the so-called "impossible trinity," which holds that a country cannot simultaneously achieve a fixed exchange rate, independent monetary policy, and high capital mobility but can only choose two of the three. In general, industrial countries
do not care about the exchange rate and are thus content with having an independent monetary policy and high capital mobility. In contrast, emerging countries are typically quite concerned about the value of the domestic currency (the
so-called "fear of floating") and use the policy rate to smooth out fluctuations in
the exchange rate, thus giving up in principle independent monetary policy. In
this light, resorting to a second instrument (that is, using reserve requirements
[RR] to do the work that the policy rate would do) may be viewed as an attempt
to return to an independent monetary policy and achieve the impossible trinity.

Why Do RR Often Serve as the Second Instrument?

Having offered a plausible rationale for a second instrument, the next question
is: what should that instrument be? Clearly, foreign exchange market
intervention cannot provide this second instrument simply because it does not
have a direct effect on output. In other words, if interest rates are raised in bad
times to defend the currency (thus worsening the accompanying recession),

there is little that foreign exchange market intervention can do to stimulate output. It is thus not surprising that, as illustrated in figure 2.12, there is a negative correlation between monetary policy and foreign exchange market intervention, which suggests that foreign exchange market intervention is pursuing the same objective of preventing the currency from depreciating (appreciating) in bad (good) times.

In contrast, RR seem a natural choice as a second instrument because, in principle, both RR and policy interest rates should have a similar effect on the economy. To illustrate this, figure 4.3 shows the effects of shocks to both instruments in the context of the four Latin America countries mentioned above. We can see (first two rows) that increases in both RR and the policy interest rate lower real GDP and increase the interest rate spread. While higher RR also reduce private credit, however, higher interest rates do not.[4] Leaving the latter anomaly aside, theory would also suggest that tighter monetary policy and higher RR should have similar effects. In Bengui, Vegh, and Vuletin (2013), for instance, an increase in reserve requirements has the standard effect of directly increasing the interest rate spread and reducing firms' demand for credit. A higher policy rate has a similar effect by raising the lending rate that banks charge to firms on account of the higher interest rate on public debt.

Which Country Characteristics Explain Different Policy Mixes?

An interesting question to ask is what country characteristics are associated with the adoption of different policy mixes. Table 4.1 addresses this particular question. This table comprises all developing countries in our sample and asks the following question: What percentage of countries that follow a particular policy mix has suffered a currency crisis during our sample period?

We can see that 36 percent of countries that follow procyclical monetary policy have had at least one currency crisis during our sample period. In contrast, just 19 percent of countries following countercyclical monetary policy have had a currency crisis. This is fully consistent with the idea that procyclical monetary policy is more likely to be present in situations in which the need to defend the currency is more pressing. On the other hand, the table also indicates that there is not a noticeable difference when it comes to the use of RR.

Table 4.2 sheds light on the relation between the level of credit and the use of RR. Specifically, it asks the question: suppose that a country follows a countercyclical RRP, what is its corresponding ratio of credit to GDP ratio? We can see that if a country follows a countercyclical RRP, its average credit to GDP ratio is 41 percent compared to just 29 percent if its RRP is acyclical.

In a similar vein, table 4.3 addresses the relationship between capital account openness and the policy mix using the Chinn-Ito index of capital account openness. It says that if a country is following countercyclical RRP, its capital account openness is considerably higher than countries that are following acyclical RRP (0.22 versus 0.09, respectively).

Figure 4.3 Relative Effect of Reserve Requirement versus Monetary Policy
The solid lines represent the response of each variable to a shock. Dashed lines represent
95% error bands

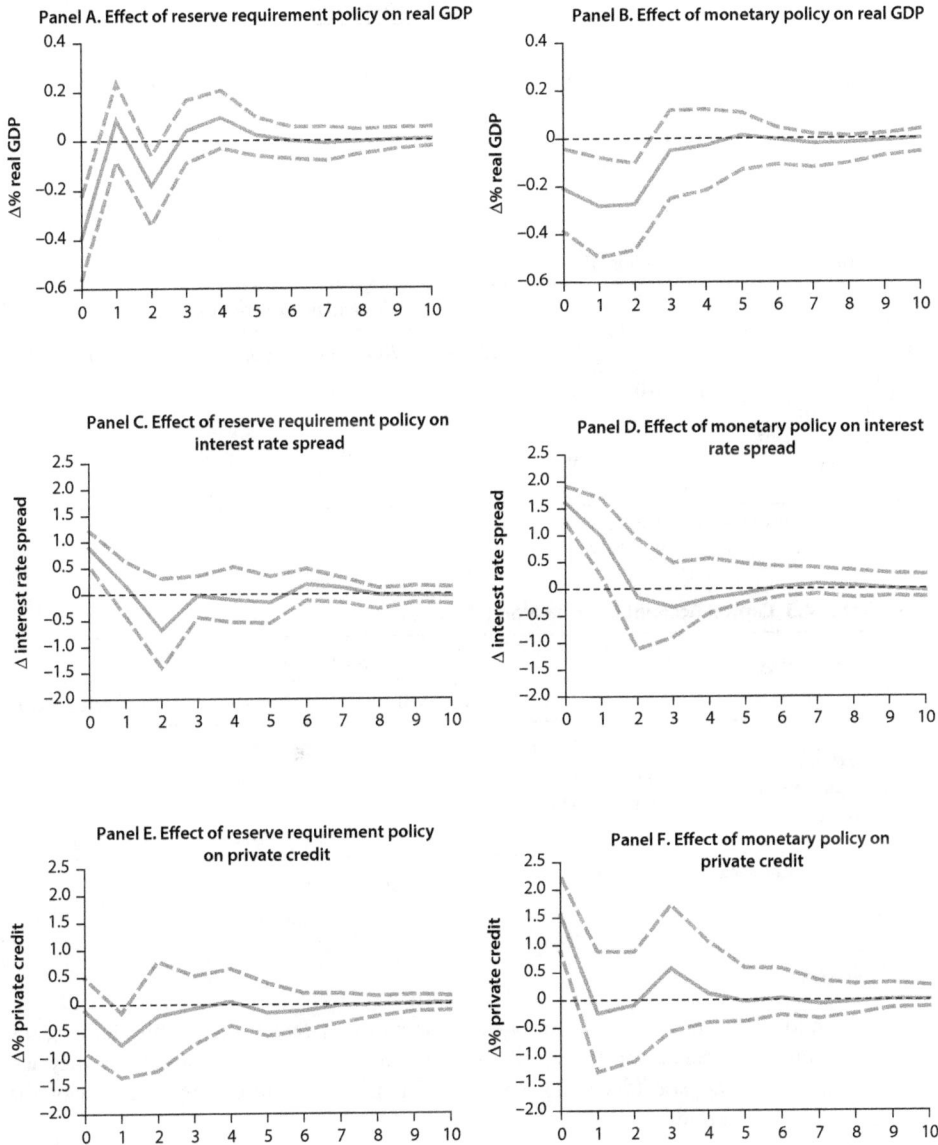

Panel A. Effect of reserve requirement policy on real GDP

Panel B. Effect of monetary policy on real GDP

Panel C. Effect of reserve requirement policy on interest rate spread

Panel D. Effect of monetary policy on interest rate spread

Panel E. Effect of reserve requirement policy on private credit

Panel F. Effect of monetary policy on private credit

Source: World Bank.
Note: Panels A and B use a four-variable panel VAR. The four variables are exogenous changes in reserve requirements, changes in central bank interest rate, real GDP growth rate, and inflation; in that order. Panels C and D use a five-variable panel VAR. The five variables are exogenous changes in reserve requirement, changes in central bank interest rate, real GDP growth rate, inflation, and interest rate spread, in that order. Interest rate spread is defined as lending minus deposit interest rates. Panels E and F use a five-variable panel VAR. The five variables are exogenous changes in reserve requirement, changes in central bank interest rate, real GDP growth rate, inflation, and private credit growth rate, in that order. Both reserve requirement and monetary (that is, central bank interest rate) shocks involve a one standard-deviation shock. Changing the order of changes in central bank interest rate does not affect qualitatively our main (cumulative) results. Dashed lines refer to 95 percent confidence intervals constructed using Monte Carlo simulations. GDP indicates gross domestic product.

Reserve Requirements in the Brave New Macroprudential World
http://dx.doi.org/10.1596/978-1-4648-0212-6

Table 4.1 Currency Crises and Policy Mix

		Central bank rate policy			
		Procyclical	*Acyclical*	*Countercyclical*	*Total*
Reserve requirement policy	**Procyclical**				
	Acyclical	0.36	0.26	0.19	0.28
	Countercyclical		0.41	0.19	0.30
	Total	0.36	0.31	0.19	

Source: Federico, Vegh, and Vuletin (2013a).

Table 4.2 Credit and Policy Mix

		Central bank rate policy			
		Procyclical	*Acyclical*	*Countercyclical*	*Total*
Reserve requirement policy	**Procyclical**				
	Acyclical	0.24	0.41	0.25	0.29
	Countercyclical		0.29	0.50	0.41
	Total	0.24	0.36	0.33	

Source: Federico, Vegh, and Vuletin (2013a).

Table 4.3 Capital Account Openness and Policy Mix

		Central bank rate policy		
		Procyclical	*Acyclical*	*Countercyclical*
Reserve requirement policy	**Procyclical**			
	Acyclical	−0.14	0.14	0.30
	Countercyclical		−0.05	0.48
	Total	−0.14	0.09	0.35

Source: Federico, Vegh, and Vuletin (2013a).

Notes

1. Following standard practice in open economy macroeconomics, we are defining the nominal exchange rate as units of domestic currency per unit of foreign currency and hence an increase (decrease) entails a nominal depreciation (appreciation) of the domestic currency.

2. While we will be thinking mainly of exchange rates as driven by the capital inflows cycle, we should note that another factor behind the negative correlation of the nominal exchange rate and real GDP could be fluctuations in commodity prices for commodity-producing emerging markets. In this scenario, a higher (lower) price of the commodity would lead to an appreciation (depreciation) of the currency. Cordella and Gupta (2014) discuss the cyclical properties of different currencies and their main determinants.

3. See Fischer (1998). Of course, many prominent economists at the time, most notably Stiglitz, raised serious questions about such a policy (see Furman and Stiglitz, 1998). More generally, the effectiveness of raising interest rates to defend the currency has

been the subject of an intense debate (see Montiel, 2003, for a detailed analysis). At a theoretical level, Hnatkovska, Lahiri, and Vegh (2008) show a model in which small increases in interest rates appreciate the currency but larger ones can actually depreciate the currency.

4. This latter result is, of course, surprising. We speculate that this result could reflect the response of both credit demand and credit supply to policy interest rates actions (Kashyap and Stein, 2000). By raising interest rate spreads, an increase in policy interest rates should reduce credit demand. However, it could also increase the bank incentives to relax other nonprice credit conditions. This later channel should, in principle, be more prevalent in economies such as the ones analyzed in this study with underdeveloped and small credit markets. Credit is measured as the percentage change in real credit.

Reserve Requirements in the Brave New Macroprudential World
http://dx.doi.org/10.1596/978-1-4648-0212-6

CHAPTER 5

Microprudential Effects of Business Cycle Management

The previous chapters have offered novel evidence about the increasing use of reserve requirements (RR) as an additional tool in policy makers' hands to cope with macroeconomic volatility. In particular, and not surprisingly, RR are more likely to be actively used when an open capital account and a procyclical currency limit the effectiveness of monetary policy in controlling credit volumes (and/or economic activity), at least for politically "acceptable" levels of the exchange rate. In other words, RR are viewed as an useful additional tool in the presence of "impossible-trinity" dilemmas; not surprisingly, countries, such as Turkey or Brazil, have used RR aggressively when they could not, or did not want to, use interest rates in a forceful manner, see box 5.1.

Box 5.1 Macroprudential Policy in Emerging Markets: The Cases of Brazil and Turkey

During late 2010-through early 2011, large capital inflows into Brazil fueled by the "real" carry trade hampered the effectiveness of monetary policy set in response to rising inflation expectations and a credit boom. The Brazilian Central Bank came to the conclusion that monetary policy alone could not address internal and external "imbalances" and decided to introduce a number of macroprudential measures to help monetary policy. In particular, it increased unremunerated RR on term deposits from 15 to 20 percent and additional remunerated RR (on demand and term deposits) from 8 to 12 percent. These measures reversed the loosening of RR that took place in late 2008 to create liquidity during the financial crisis. In addition, to curb credit growth, the tax on financial operations (IOF) was raised from 1.5 to 3.0 percent (annualized), and applied to credit operations for individuals, on a daily basis, for a maximum of one year. Capital requirements for consumer loan were also increased through a change in risk weights: for the fast-growing segment of vehicle financing, the

box continues next page

Box 5.1 Macroprudential Policy in Emerging Markets: The Cases of Brazil and Turkey *(continued)*

weight was increased from 75 to 150 percent, which was equivalent to an increase in capital requirement of 8 to 16.5 percent. At the same time, in order to avoid the build-up of excessive maturity mismatches (in Brazil, bank liabilities have very short maturity and/or duration) the loan to value ratio (LTV) on vehicle loans was increased, penalizing longer maturities—the maximum LTV was set to 80 percent for loans between 24 and 36 months, to 70 for loans between 36 and 48 months, and to 60 percent for loans between 48 and 60. Finally, in order to curb the carry trade, the IOF on nonresident portfolio investments was increased from 2 to 4 percent (and ultimately to 6) and a 60 percent unremunerated RR on banks' short position in the forex spot market was imposed; additional measures were also adopted to limit banks' exposure in forex derivative markets. In 2012, faced with less favorable global conditions, the central bank adjusted the macroprudential stance reducing the additional RR on demand deposits from 12 to 6 percent first and then to zero, and the additional RR on time deposits from 12 to 11 percent. Finally, in the summer of 2013, confronted with strong currency depreciation pressures triggered by the Federal Reserve's "tapering talks," the IOF on forex operation was abolished; in December 2013, the IOF on cash withdrawals in foreign countries was increased from 0.38 to 6.38 percent.

Faced with policy dilemmas similar to Brazil's, Turkey also relied heavily on macroprudential measures. RR changed very frequently. For instance, the RR on short-term foreign currency deposits was reduced from 6 to 5 percent during the financial crisis and then was progressively increased up to 16 percent, only to be reduced again to the current 11.5 percent. RR for domestic currency deposits followed a similar pattern. In addition to the active use of RR—which on occasions moved in the opposite direction to the policy interest rate to contain the appreciation of the exchange rate and the cost of sterilized foreign exchange interventions—the Central Bank of Turkey allowed banks to satisfy a certain share of their RR for domestic currency deposits with foreign exchange or gold; interestingly, such a share has become an additional policy tool in the hands of the monetary authorities. Finally, during 2011, the Banking Regulation and Supervision Agency took a number of measures meant to prevent the build-up of excessive risk in the expansionary phase of the cycle. In addition to an (implicit) 25 percent nominal credit growth ceiling communicated to banks (relying on moral suasion), LTV ceilings on real estate loans were implemented; risk weights on consumer loans were increased (from 100 to 150 percent on maturities below two years, and from 100 to 200 percent on longer maturities); larger provisions were required for such loans and restrictions were imposed on the increase in credit cards limits for consumers with large outstanding credit.

Sources: Pereira da Silva and Harris 2013; Central Bank of Brazil; IMF 2012; Central Bank of Turkey.

Few would disagree with the fact that, by smoothing the business cycle, the countercyclical use of RR has the potential to smooth out the business cycle and reduce the build-up of systemic risk in an economy. However, less is known about how RR or other prudential tools such as capital requirements, limits on LTV, and so forth affect individual institutions' risk-taking incentives. In other words, what are the microprudential properties of the different macroprudential tools?

Tradeoffs over the Business Cycle

In order to properly assess how the use of different macroprudential tools may affect individual banks' risk-taking incentives, we need to move away from the standard modelling of macroprudential policies in the Dynamic Stochastic General Equilibrium (DSGE) literature that, due to just focusing on externalities, ends up treating all prudential instruments as alternative forms of Pigouvian taxation. Different prudential instruments do affect financial intermediaries' incentives to take on risk differently and, in certain instances, the micro- and macroprudential properties of specific policies may not go hand in hand.

To be able to discuss some of the trade-offs that regulators may face along the business cycle,[1] it is important to focus on a few critical distortions that justify the presence of an active prudential regulation. More precisely, we should keep in mind that: (1) because of limited liability, individual banks take on excessive risk; (2) because of deposit insurance, they opt for cheap, short-term, and unstable sources of funds, transferring to the public the cost of liquidity insurance; and (3) because of externalities, they do not internalize the effect of (i) their lending policies on the stability of the financial system (and tend to lend too much in good times and too little in bad times), (ii) they do not internalize the effects of their funding strategy on other banks' liquidity risk.

In the current jargon, the first two distortions call for microprudential policies, and the third for macroprudential ones. Of course, this categorization, like all categorizations, is somehow arbitrary. However, it could be helpful in understanding different rationales for the countercyclical use of prudential measures. We will start by taking the macroprudential policy stance as given and will discuss in more depth the possible trade-offs at the end of the section.

Building on Cordella and Pienknagura (2013), we now discuss whether macroprudential policies implemented either through RR (as discussed in previous sections), through countercyclical capital requirements as in Spain, Colombia, and Peru,[2] or through other forms of taxation may affect individual banks' risk-taking incentives.

We will start our analysis by focusing on the microprudential dimension in order to understand how individual banks' risk-taking incentives may vary across the credit cycle. When the credit cycle is driven by the project cycle, that is, if it is driven by the relative abundance or scarcity of quality projects, then banks tend to be naturally prudent on the upside not to lose their profit opportunities. This suggests that tensions may arise between the stances of macro and microprudential policies and that the regulator should carefully assess the nature of the financial frictions (principal agents versus externalities) in order to properly set the policy stance. This finding is not as surprising as one may think, and there is plenty of evidence that in periods of economic boom (that is, when there is abundance of good projects, or at least of projects perceived as good) supervisors are usually satisfied with the levels of banks' capital and provisions while, in period of downturns, they become more worried and may ask for remedial actions which, from a macroprudential perspective, may make things worse.

Reserve Requirements in the Brave New Macroprudential World
http://dx.doi.org/10.1596/978-1-4648-0212-6

When the cycle is driven by the cost of financing, instead, risk taking tends to be procyclical. The reason is that, as Dell'Ariccia, Leaven, and Marquez (2014) show in a recent paper, easy financing conditions (low interest rates) reduce the benefits of holding capital (to reduce the agency problems associated with limited liabilities) and thus foster higher leverage and additional risk taking. While this is true when banks optimally choose their capital level,[3] if banks are undercapitalized, the risk shifting channel becomes predominant and the classical Stiglitz and Weiss' (1981) result that high interest rates lead to riskier behavior may still hold true. While macro and microprudential policies may go hand in hand when the cycle is driven by the interest rate, this "synchronicity" is more likely if banks are well capitalized. In situations in which leverage is substantial, for instance because of implicit bailout guarantees, conflicts between the macro- and micropolicy stances may instead still arise.

The next step is to look at the effects of different macroprudential instruments on banks' risk taking incentives. Of course, the tightening of macroprudential regulation—through an increase in minimum capital requirements, RR, or taxes on credit—leads to a reduction in credit volumes. However, while an increase in capital requirements decreases the riskiness of the banks' loan portfolio, an increase in RR or taxes on credit is likely to increase it.

How does this happen? The reason is that an increase in the banks' external cost of funding, driven by an increase in RR, affects the banks' bottom line only in those states of the world in which the bank actually repays its debt, that is, when it does not fail. This means that higher RR reduce the banks' returns in the case of success and thus make banks less willing to put an additional effort to improve the quality of their portfolio. In other words, higher RR tend to exacerbate moral hazard and to induce banks to behave in a less prudent way. The idea that RR have a negative effect on the risk taking incentives of banks is not new to policy makers. Indeed, Aldo Mendes, the Brazil Central Bank's director responsible for monetary policy, recently stated that "lowering reserve requirements helps financial stability."[4] The practical argument, highlighted in a recent International Monetary Fund (IMF) (2012) report, is that "unlike an increase in capital requirements, an increase in RRs has no impact on the resilience of the banking system to loan losses [...] When RRs squeeze profitability, this can lead banks to shift into higher margin, but higher risk segments, in an effort to restore return on equity" (p. 15). As an example, the report mentions the unwanted consequences (on risk taking) of Turkey's aggressive RR increase in early 2011.

Notice that even with the absence of deposit insurance, that is, when banks have an incentive to raise additional capital to reduce their cost of funding, they will nonetheless be prone to take on excessive risk (as compared to the social optimal levels) as long as they cannot credibly commit to a given level of portfolio risk. Of course, if the regulator has to act on behalf of less sophisticated (small) depositors and/or the deposit insurer, then it will have to further tighten prudential norms and raise capital requirements to re-equilibrate the incentives that were additionally perturbed by the presence of public guarantees.

What we are arguing here is not that RR are bad instruments per se. They are powerful macrostabilization tools that help monetary policies in the presence of volatile capital flows. Also, RR together with other prudential measures targeting the liability structure of the banking sector, such as the net stable funding ratio introduced in Basel III, could strengthen the resilience of the financial system to liquidity shocks. Instead, what we are trying to stress here is that there can be trade-offs between instruments. What stabilizes liquidity or reduces aggregate risk may have negative consequences on the risk-taking incentives of individual banks.

Looking at the trade-offs over the business cycle, our view is that the cyclical use of taxes to dampen the credit cycle may exacerbate the tensions between micro- and macroprudential policies when the cycle is driven by interest rates. When interest rates are low, banks already have an incentive to move to riskier projects and incentives are strengthened if liabilities are heavily taxed. When, instead, the cycle is driven by a great abundance of good projects, banks tend to be more prudent and the adverse effect of RR (or other form of "taxes") on banks' incentives is partially offset by the prudent behavior fostered by the stronger demand for credit.

If, instead of taxes, capital requirements are the instruments used to deal with the business cycle, there is no major structural conflict between micro- and macroprudential measures. A tightening of capital requirements reduces both aggregate risk and individual banks' risk-taking incentives. However, there can still be cyclical tensions between micro- and macro objectives, when the cycle is driven by the quality of good projects. In this case, capital requirements have to be countercyclical for macroprudential reasons but not for microprudential reasons.

When we look at the interaction between monetary policy and capital requirements, the picture is much more nuanced one. In particular, capital requirements may make monetary policy more microprudential friendly. Indeed, the effect of monetary policy tightening on banks' risk taking may depend on the level of capital requirements. For low levels of capital requirements, an interest rate hike increases the riskiness of bank's loan portfolio, while the opposite is true if capital requirements are sufficiently high. The intuition is simple: monetary policy affects the incentives of banks in two ways: (i) by decreasing the returns in the case of success (since the increase in the cost of funding is only partially passed on to borrowers), and (ii) by increasing the banks' skin in the game. When capital requirements are low, the first effect dominates, and this leads risk taking to follow the interest rate. Instead, when capital requirements are sufficiently high, the latter effect dominates, and interest rate hikes make banks behave more prudently. This is the same argument as in Dell'Ariccia et al. (2014) who, as we discussed above, show that if the capital structure of the bank is fixed the effect of a monetary easing on risk taking depends on banks' leverage.

Finally, in order to have a more comprehensive understanding of some additional possible trade-offs between macro and macroprudential policies it is useful to look at the how banks' incentives are affected by the amplitude and the persistence of the business cycle. From a macroprudential perspective a persistent

Reserve Requirements in the Brave New Macroprudential World
http://dx.doi.org/10.1596/978-1-4648-0212-6

positive aggregate shock is expected to relax collateral constraints, increase leverage, and, via externalities, induce excessive euphoria and risk taking. On the other hand, negative and prolonged negative shocks will put a dent on financial intermediaries' net worth, tighten collateral constraints, and induce downward spirals marked by massive fire sales and deleveraging. The avoidance of such boom and bust cycles fueled by externalities is indeed the main objective of macroprudential policies.

From a pure microprudential perspective the effects of the persistence and the amplitude of the business cycle are more complex and may deserve additional investigation. Cordella and Pienknagura (2014) argue that the volatility of credit demand increases monitoring effort and that this effect is stronger when shocks' persistence is low. The fact that an increase in the amplitude of demand fluctuations increases monitoring may at first look surprising, but it should not. It is the consequence of a well-established result, proved by Oi (1961), that demand fluctuations increase firms' profits. In their framework, this implies that expected profits in case of success increase with the volatility of demand and so do the returns associated with monitoring. This is what makes banks behave more prudently at equilibrium. These results provide additional evidence that, from a microprudential perspective, there is no reason to assume that higher volatility in the economic environment necessary leads to more risk taking. Furthermore, when the business cycle is driven by the project cycle, conflicts between the micro- and macroprudential stances are to be expected.

Note

1. The focus of this section is to discuss the policy trade-offs that may arise between different instruments when prudential regulation has to be adjusted along the business cycle. In other words, we focus on changes rather than on levels.

2. For a comprehensive discussion of these experiences, see Fernández de Lis and García-Herrero (2013).

3. This effect is relevant independently of the presence of a deposit guarantee, but is magnified if the latter is in place.

4. Bloomberg, September 20, 2012.

CHAPTER 6

Policy Tensions and Tradeoffs

The idea that the overall design of macroprudential policies should start from a careful analysis of the role that different financial frictions play in different environments (or in different moment of the business cycle) is discussed in great depth by de la Torre and Ize (2013).[1] In particular, the authors focus their attention on how the introduction of asymmetric information, externalities, bounded rationality, and mood swings in a standard Arrow-Debreu model lead to different policy implications. In particular, they emphasize that when focusing on the different transmission channels it becomes clear that not all financial fluctuations, however large and procyclical, and not all financial crises, however painful, justify preventive macroprudential policy.

Given that similar symptoms can reflect very different underlying forces, suitable policy responses require a reasonable sense of what is behind the observed financial turbulence, whether the inefficiencies are mainly driven by policy failures or market failures and, in the latter case, whether the relevant market failures reflect mainly public moral hazard, substantial externalities that rational players do not internalize, or irrational mood swings driven by noise traders.

Finding a proper balance in macroprudential policy is further complicated by tensions and trade-offs in policy impacts when different kind of financial frictions occur simultaneously. For example, penalizing short-term wholesale funding may be good to deal with collective action failures (it induces the internalization of externalities associated with systemic runs and liquidity risk) but can exacerbate agency failures (it weakens the ability of principals to discipline agents by holding them on a "tight leash"). Mark-to-market requirements can have similarly conflicting impacts—they help markets cope with principal-agent frictions but can magnify contagious runs or spur irrational mood swings.

Moreover, macroprudential policies aimed at addressing systemic risks in a collective action domain can act as a common factor (or as an aggregate shock) inasmuch as they affect financial intermediaries and financial contracts across the board. Hence, they may require countervailing macroprudential policies under an agency domain to offset the incentive distortions that the former can produce. For example, as we have discussed in the previous section, a Pigouvian tax or liquidity requirement that penalizes short-term funding under a collective-action rationale of macroprudential policy may undermine individual banks' incentives, thereby requiring an offsetting boost in capital requirements because of micro-prudential concerns.

More generally, the policy balance will also depend on the type of error one wishes to minimize. Policy makers that perceive credit dynamics and market forces to be strongly self-stabilizing might prefer to minimize type I error—that is, avoid overregulating markets or undermining market discipline, even if that implies an occasional systemic crisis. However, policy makers that perceive a large scope for collective action and cognition failures might prefer to minimize type II error—that is, prevent devastating systemic crises, even if that implies sacrificing financial market discipline and efficiency.

Given these constraints, two broad macroprudential policy options can be envisaged. One option is to assemble an all-terrain regulatory framework. However, this may lead to policy inconsistencies and regulatory arbitrage, and end up being too inflexible to deal with large and relatively rapid changes in systemic risk buildup. The alternative is to develop a state-contingent (bimodal) regulatory framework that focuses in normal times on market discipline and the classic agency frictions but shifts in exceptional times (of bubble formation or bubble bursts) to a focus on systemic risk and the destabilizing role of collective action and cognition frictions. This option presupposes, however, that the normal-times oversight is effective enough to detect fault lines in the financial system before it is too late, and that the regulator is sufficiently independent, objective, and agile to switch to exceptional-times prudential oversight when warranted.

Progress towards bridging the gap between theory and practice will therefore require better identifying the main frictions and failures at work, formally incor-porating them in theoretical models, assessing their welfare impact, and sorting out constrained efficiencies from constrained inefficiencies. This effort will need to be accompanied by further empirical efforts to estimate and calibrate the net impact of regulations, while at the same time gauging their unintended side effects.

Notes

1. This section draws very heavily on chapter 6 of this paper.

CHAPTER 7

Policy Conclusions

Several important conclusions and policy lessons follow from this report:

- We find a very different behavior in industrial and emerging countries regarding the use of macroprudential policy (at least in terms of reserve requirements [RR]). Since 2004, in particular, no industrial country has resorted to active RR policy, whereas close to half of developing countries have, of which 90 percent have used RR countercyclically.
- RR seem to be an important component of a trio of policy instruments (together with short-term interest rates and foreign exchange market intervention) that developing countries have relied on for several decades now as they go through boom-bust cycles mainly induced by international capital flows. Despite all the buzz about systemic risk-driven macroprudential policy, we found no evidence of such use of RR in industrial countries.
- The genesis for resorting to RR lies essentially on the behavior of the exchange rate over the business cycle in developing countries (with the currency depreciating in bad times and appreciating in good times). This complicates enormously the use of interest rates as a countercyclical instrument because doing so would appreciate (depreciate) even more the currency in good (bad) times.
- The evidence suggests that RR are an effective instrument (that is, a rise in RR increases the interest rate spread and reduces credit and gross domestic product [GDP]) that can well be used countercyclically when concerns about the effects of interest rates on the exchange rate become paramount.
- It may well be the case that—and this is what we observe in countries such as Chile where policy institutions have improved steadily over time—developing countries may reach a point in time where it may no longer be necessary to use RR as a business cycle-driven macroprudential policy. Until then, however, RR seem a natural and effective instrument to complement monetary policy.
- Even if and when a given developing country may reach a point where RR are no longer necessary as a part of the policy mix, RR may still be optimal to use

as systemic risk-driven macroprudential policy. Our report, however, does not speak to the effectiveness of RR as a risk-reducing prudential instrument and therefore future research is called for in this regard.

- While from a macroprudential point of view, the most common prudential instruments are essentially equivalent (for instance, RR, capital requirements, and taxes on credit), from a microprudential point of view they may elicit very different responses regarding banks' risk taking behavior over the business cycle.
- Depending on the nature and the drivers of the business cycle, conflicts may arise between the micro- and macroprudential policy stances.
- The overall design of macroprudential policies should follow a careful analysis of the role that different financial frictions play in different environments since similar symptoms can reflect very different underlying forces.
- More research is needed to embed banks' risk-taking incentives in macroeconomic models in order to properly assess and quantify the tensions that may arise between micro- and macroprudential policies and to design a coherent prudential framework for the financial system.

Bibliography

Bengui, Julien, Carlos Vegh, and Guillermo Vuletin. 2013. "Fixed Costs in Banking and the Optimal Mix of Reserve Requirement and Interest Rate Policy." Unpublished manuscript.

Blanchard, Olivier, and Roberto Perotti. 2002. "An Empirical Characterization of the Dynamic Effects of Changes in Government Spending and Taxes on Output." *The Quarterly Journal of Economics* 117: 1329–68.

Bulow, Jeremy, John Geanakoplos, and Paul Klemperer. 1985. "Multimarket Oligopoly: Strategic Substitutes and Strategic Complements." *Journal of Political Economy* 93: 488–511.

Calvo, Guillermo, Leonardo Leiderman, and Carmen M. Reinhart. 1993. "Capital Inflows and Real Exchange Rate Appreciation in Latin America: The Role of External Factors." *IMF Staff Papers* 40: 108–51.

Coibion, Olivier. 2012. "Are the Effects of Monetary Policy Shocks Big or Small?" *American Economic Journal: Macroeconomics* 4: 1–32.

Cordella, Tito, and Poonam Gupta. 2014. "What Makes a Currency Procyclical: An Empirical Investigation." Unpublished manuscript.

Cordella, Tito, and Samuel Pienknagura. 2013. "Macro Prudential Policies from a Micro Prudential Angle." World Policy Research Working Paper No 6721, World Bank, Washington, DC.

———. 2014. "Bank Risk Taking over the Business Cycle." Unpublished manuscript.

Coulibaly, Brahima. 2012. "Monetary Policy in Emerging Market Economies: What Lessons from the Global Financial Crisis." International Finance Discussion Paper No. 1042, Board of Governors of the Federal Reserve System, Washington, DC.

de la Torre, Augusto, and Ize, Alain. 2013. "The Foundations of Macroprudential Regulation: A Conceptual Roadmap." Policy Research Working Paper Series No 6575, World Bank, Washington, DC.

Dell'Ariccia, Giovanni, Luc Leaven, and Robert Marquez. 2014. "Monetary Policy, Leverage, and Bank Risk Taking." *Journal of Economic Theory* 149: 65–99.

Diaz-Alejandro, Carlos. 1985. "Good-bye Financial Repression, Hello Financial Crash." *Journal of Development Economics* 19: 1–24.

Federico, Pablo, Carlos Vegh, and Guillermo Vuletin. 2013a. "Reserve Requirement Policy over the Business Cycle." Unpublished manuscript.

———. 2013b. "Effects and Role of Macroprudential Policy: Evidence from Reserve Requirements Based on a Narrative Approach." Unpublished manuscript.

———. 2013c. "Macroprudential Policies in Brazil and Mexico from 1970 to 2010."
Unpublished manuscript.

Fernández de Lis, Santiago, and Alicia García-Herrero. 2013. "Dynamic Provisioning:
Some Lessons from Existing Experiences."*Economia* 13: 35–60.

Fischer, Stanley. 1998. "The IMF and the Asian crisis." Forum Funds Lecture at UCLA
(1998).

Flood, Robert, and Olivier Jeanne. 2005. "An Interest Rate Defense of a Fixed Exchange
Rate?" *Journal of International Economics* 66: 471–84.

Frankel, Jeffrey. 2011. "A Solution to Fiscal Procyclicality: The Structural Budget
Institutions Pioneered by Chile." NBER Working Paper no. 16945, National Bureau of
Economic Research, Cambridge, MA.

Frankel, Jeffrey, Carlos Vegh, and Guillermo Vuletin. 2013. "On Graduation from Fiscal
Policy Procyclicality." *Journal of Development Economics* 100: 32–47.

Furman, Jason, and Joseph Stiglitz. 1998. "Economic Crises: Evidence and Insights from
East Asia." *Brookings Papers on Economic Activity* 2: 1–135.

Glocker, Christian, and Pascal Towbin. 2012. "The Macroeconomic Effects of Reserve
Requirements." WIFO Working Paper No. 420, Banque de France, Paris.

Hnatkovska, Viktoria, Amartya Lahiri, and Carlos Vegh. 2008. "Interest Rates and the
Exchange Rate: A Non-monotonic Tale." NBER Working Paper No. 13925, National
Bureau of Economic Research, Cambridge, MA.

IMF (International Monetary Fund). 2012. "The Interaction of Monetary and
Macroprudential Policies." IMF Policy Paper.

Kashyap, Anil, and Jeremy C. Stein. 2000. "What Do a Million Observations on Banks Say
about the Transmission of Monetary Policy?"*American Economic Review* 90: 407–28.

Lahiri, Amartya, and Carlos Vegh. 2003. "Delaying the Inevitable: Interest Rate Defense
and Balance of Payments Crises." *Journal of Political Economy* 111: 404–24.

McKinnon, Ronald I. 1973. *Money and Capital in Economic Development*. Washington,
DC: Brookings Institution.

Montiel, Peter. 2003. "Tight Money in a Post-crisis Defense of the Exchange Rate: What
Have We Learned?" *The World Bank Research Observer*. 18: 1–23.

Oi, Walter. 1961. "The Desirability of Price Instability Under Perfect Competition."
Econometrica 29: 58–64.

Pereira da Silva, Luiz, and Ricardo Harris. 2013. "Sailing through the Global Financial
Storm." In *Dealing with the Challenges of Macro Financial Linkages in Emerging
Markets*, edited by Otaviano Canuto and Swati Ghosh. World Bank Study. Washington,
DC: World Bank.

Riera-Crichton, Daniel, Carlos Vegh, and Guillermo Vuletin. 2012. "Tax Multipliers:
Pitfalls in Measurement and Identification." NBER Working Paper No 18497, National
Bureau of Economic Research, Cambridge, MA.

Romer, Christina, and David Romer. 2004. "A New Measure of Monetary Shocks:
Derivation and Implications." *American Economic Review* 94: 1055–84.

———. 2010. "The Macroeconomic Effects of Tax Changes: Estimates Based on a New
Measure of Fiscal Shocks." *American Economic Review* 100 (3): 763–801.

Shaw, Edward. 1973. *Financial Deepening in Economic Development*. New York: Oxford
University Press.

Stiglitz, Joseph, and Andrew Weiss. 1981. "Credit Rationing in Markets with Imperfect Information." *The American Economic Review* 71: 393–410.

Tovar, Camilo, Mercedes Garcia-Escribano, and Mercedes Vera Martin. 2012. "Credit Growth and the Effectiveness of Reserve Requirements and Other Macroprudential Instruments in Latin America." IMF Working Paper No. 142.

Vegh, Carlos, and Guillermo Vuletin. 2013. "Overcoming the Fear of Free Falling: Monetary Policy Graduation in Emerging Markets." In *The Role of Central Banks in Financial Stability: How Has It Changed?* edited by Douglas Evanoff, Cornelia Holthausen, George Kaufman, and Manfred Kremer. Federal Reserve Bank of Chicago and European Central Bank 105–31.

Environmental Benefits Statement

The World Bank is committed to reducing its environmental footprint. In support of this commitment, the Publishing and Knowledge Division leverages electronic publishing options and print-on-demand technology, which is located in regional hubs worldwide. Together, these initiatives enable print runs to be lowered and shipping distances decreased, resulting in reduced paper consumption, chemical use, greenhouse gas emissions, and waste.

The Publishing and Knowledge Division follows the recommended standards for paper use set by the Green Press Initiative. Whenever possible, books are printed on 50 percent to 100 percent postconsumer recycled paper, and at least 50 percent of the fiber in our book paper is either unbleached or bleached using Totally Chlorine Free (TCF), Processed Chlorine Free (PCF), or Enhanced Elemental Chlorine Free (EECF) processes.

More information about the Bank's environmental philosophy can be found at http://crinfo.worldbank.org/wbcrinfo/node/4.

green press INITIATIVE

www.ingramcontent.com/pod-product-compliance
Lightning Source LLC
Chambersburg PA
CBHW081513200326
41518CB00015B/2482